Now I Know!

1 Learning to read

Student Book

Tessa Lochowski and Mary Roulston

Contents

1

What do we find in schools?

Listening
- I can understand simple instructions.

Speaking
- I can answer simple questions about things at school.
- I can name things in the classroom.

4

1  Look and say. What's in your classroom?

2 Look at the picture. Find and check (✓).

☐ ☐ ☐

3  **BBC** Watch the video. Check (✓) and color.
1-1

English Class

☐ ☐ ☐

☐ ☐ ☐

☐ ☐ ☐

Vocabulary 1

1 🎧 1-02 **Listen and repeat.**

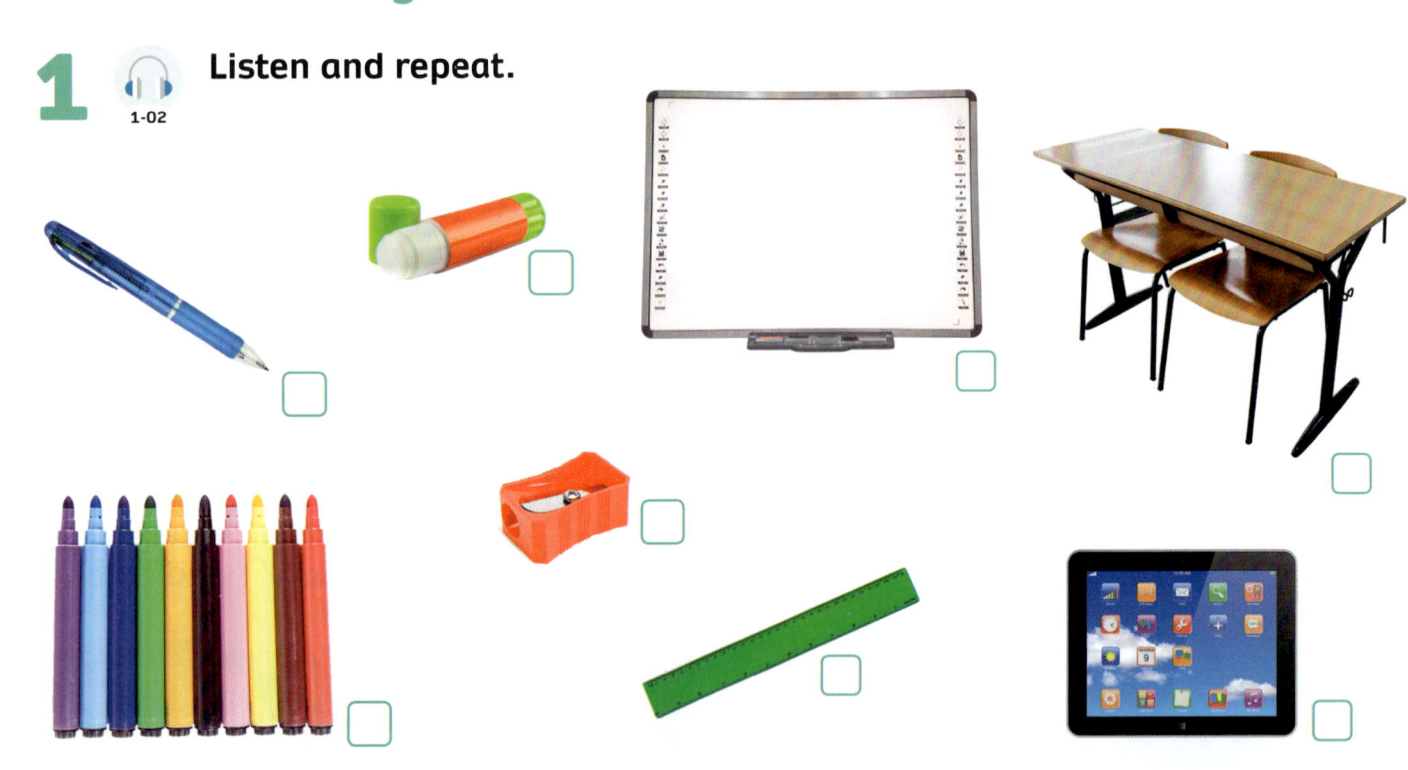

2 🎧 1-03 **Listen and number.**

3 🎧 1-04 **Listen and say.**

4 💬 **Find and match. Then say.**

1

2

3

4

5

6

5  **Watch the video on classrooms again. What can you see?**

6 **Draw and say. What's in your pencil case?**

Story 1

1 **Look at the picture.
What can you see?**

2 **Think! What's in the story?
Check (✓).**

Story 1

3 1-05 **Listen. Check your answers from Activity 2.**

SCHOOLS AROUND the World

1

4  1-06 **Listen again. Check (✓) or cross (X).**

1

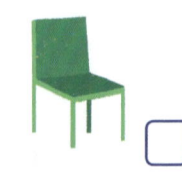 ☐    ☐    ☐

3

 ☐    ☐    ☐

2

 ☐    ☐    ☐

4

 ☐   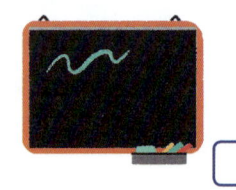 ☐   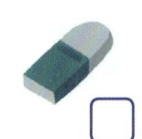 ☐

5  **Talk with a friend. What's in your classroom?**

Grammar 1

1   **Watch Part 1 of the story video. Where's Tommy?**

2 1-07 **Listen and check (✓). What's in Albert's classroom?**

3 1-08 **Listen and repeat.**

1   2   3   4   5

4 **Look at the pictures. Ask and answer.**

5 **Listen and repeat.**
1-09

6 **Think and say. Then listen and number.**
1-10

 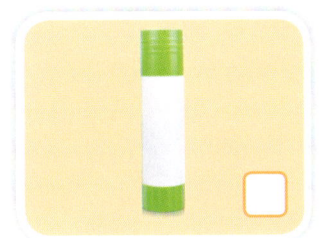  

Speaking

7  **Work in pairs. Ask and answer about things in your classroom.**

Vocabulary 2

1 1-11 **Listen and repeat.**

2  1-12 **Listen. Find and check (✓).**

3 1-13 **Listen and say.**

4  **Where are we? Look and say.**

5  What's in your school? Think and say.

6 Look at the pictures. What can you do? Check (✓).

Story 2

1 Look at the pictures. What can you see?

Story 2

2 🎧 1-14 Listen to the story. Find the pictures from Activity 1.

First Day

14

3 1-15 **Listen to the story again. Check (✓).**

4 **Think about the first day at school. Tell your friend.**

 ☹ ☐

☺ ☐

☺ ☐

 15

Grammar 2

1   **Watch Part 1 of the story video. What does Miss Sparks say?**

2 Listen and repeat.
1-16

1 2 3 4 Speak English

3 Listen and number.
1-17

Listening and Speaking

4 **1-18** **Listen and do.**

5 **Work with a friend. Do a picture dictation.**

6  **1-3** **B B C** **Watch Part 2 of the story video. Who's Dan? Check (✓).**

7  **1-4** **B B C** **Watch Part 3 of the story video. What's in Tommy's backpack? Check (✓).**

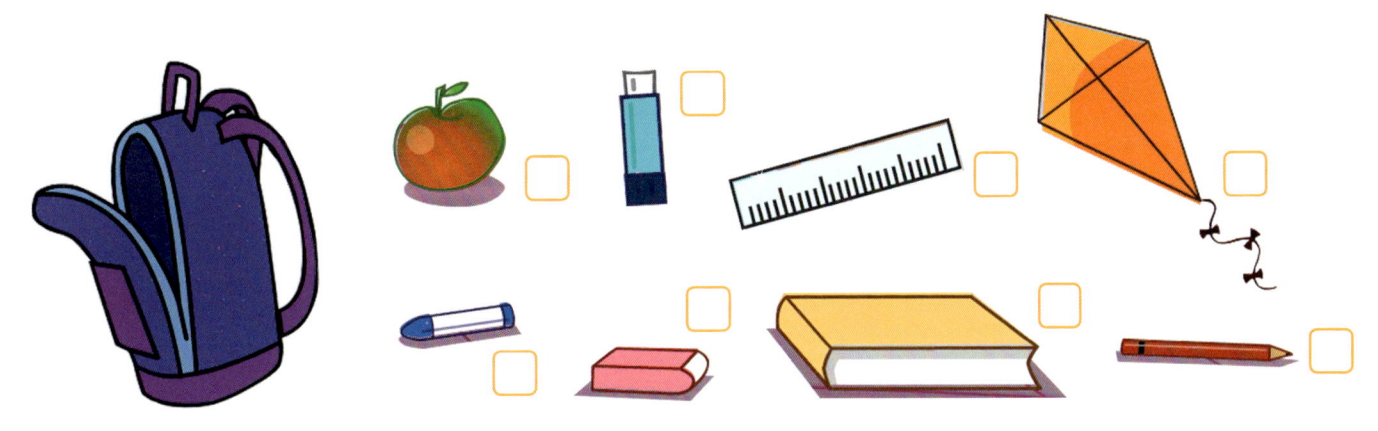

Phonics

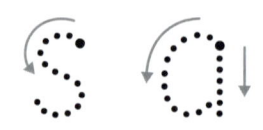

1 🎧 1-19 **Listen and repeat. Then trace.**

2 🎧 1-20 **Listen and check (✓) in blue (s) or in red (a).**

3 💬 **Say the words. Check (✓) the odd one out.**

1

2

3

4

4 💬 **Draw and say.**

a

s

18

Now I Know

1 **Draw and say.**

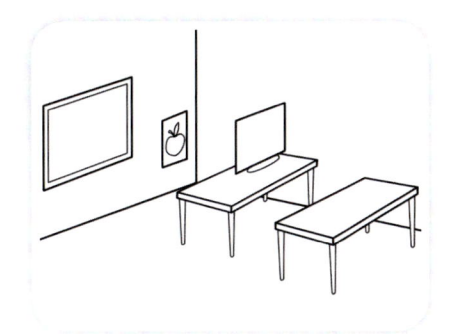

2 **Choose a project.**

| Draw your classroom. | **or** | Make a classroom rules poster. |

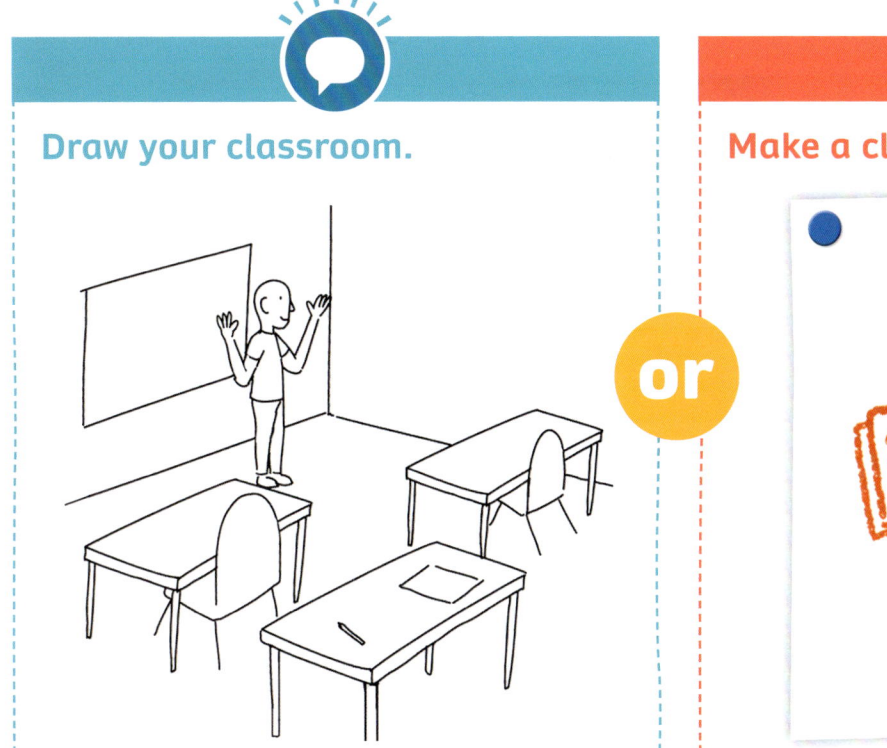

★ ★ ★ ★   Color the stars   ★ ★ ★ ★

 I can understand simple instructions.

 I can answer simple questions about things at school.

 I can name things in the classroom.

2

Where do we see shapes and colors?

Listening

- I can understand simple questions about things around me.

Speaking

- I can name simple shapes and colors.

1 Say the colors. Can you see them in your classroom?

2 Look at the picture. Find and say the colors.

3 2-1 BBC Watch the video. What do you see? Check (✓).

Vocabulary 1

1 **1-21** **Listen and repeat.**

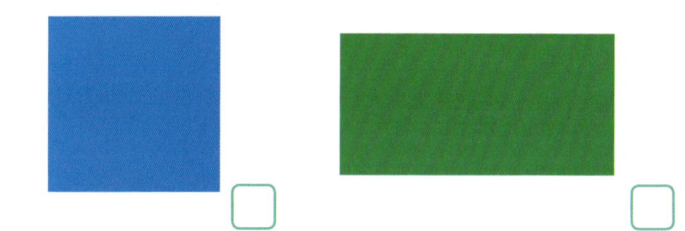

   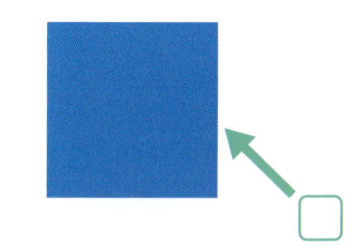

2 **1-22** **Listen and number.**

3 **1-23** **Listen again. Say.**

4 **How many sides? Draw.**

1 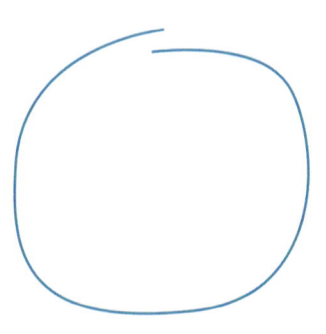	3
4	5

5 2-1  **Watch the video on shapes again. Say the shapes.**

6 **Match. Say the shapes.**

1

2

3

4

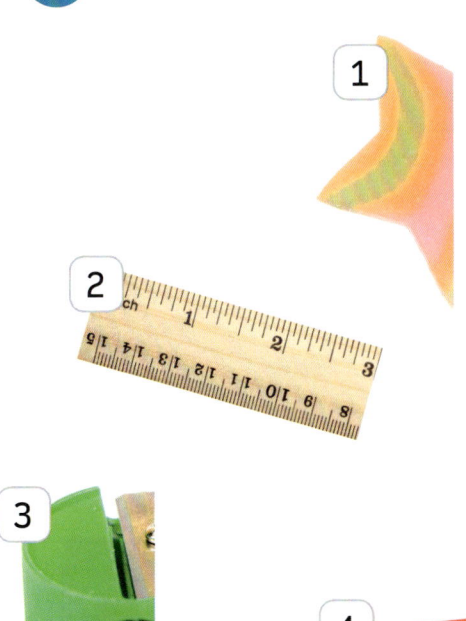

Story 1

1 **Look. What can you see?**

Let's Go on a Shape Hunt

1

Story 1

2 🎧 1-24 **Listen to the story. Find the pictures from Activity 1.**

2

3

4

3 🎧 **Listen and check (✓).**

1-25

1

2

3

4

4 💬 **Talk with a friend. What shapes and colors are in your neighborhood?** ❓

Grammar 1

1  **Watch Part 1 of the story video. What colors can you see?**

2 **Watch Part 2 of the story video. Say the shapes you hear.**

3 **Listen and check (✓). Then repeat.**

4 **Color the kites. Ask and answer.**

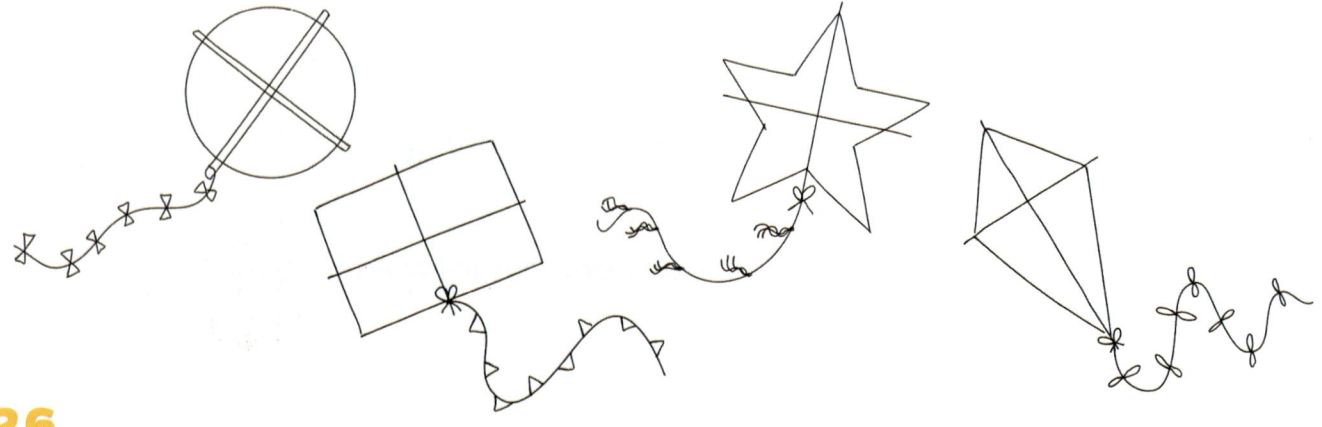

5 🎧 1-27 Listen and check (✓).

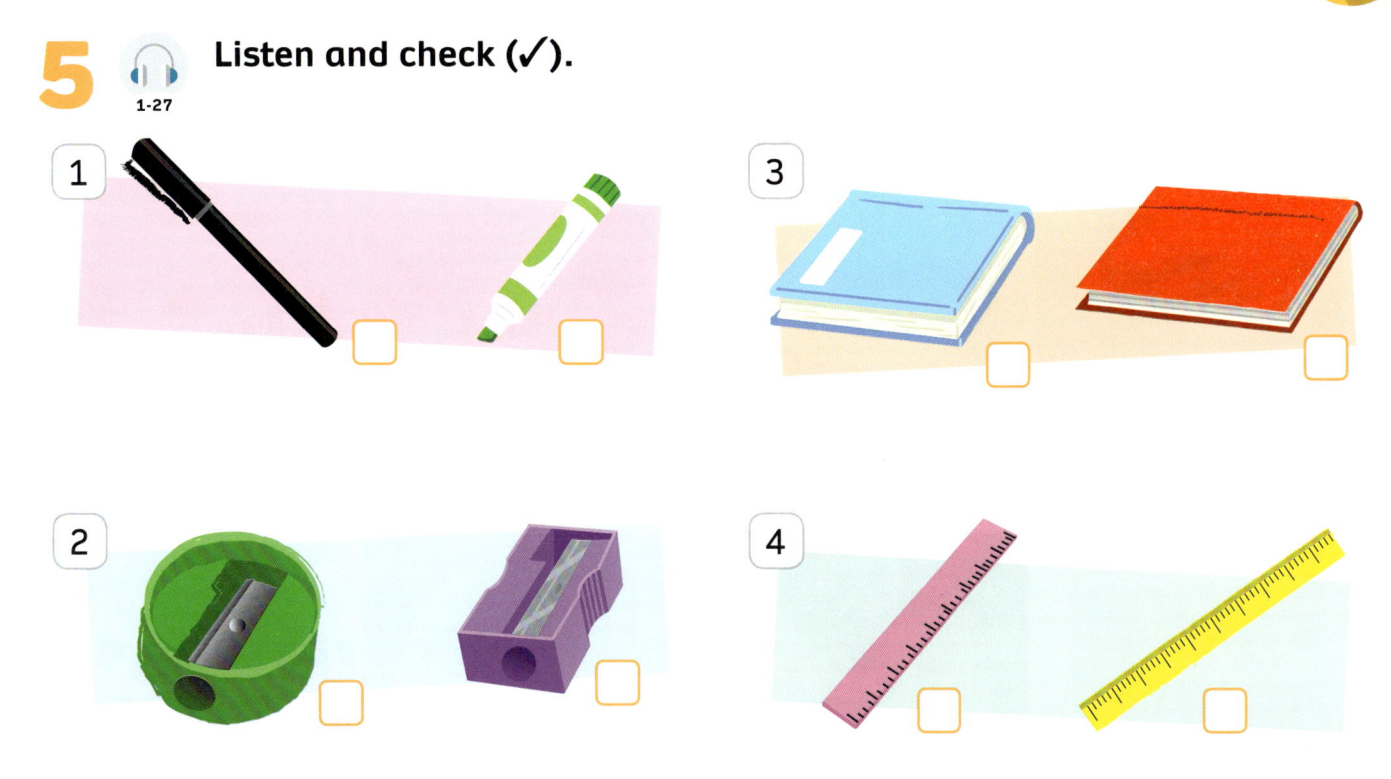

1

2

3

4

Listening and Speaking 1

6 🎧 1-28 Listen. Then ask and answer with a friend.

Vocabulary 2

1 1-29 **Listen and repeat.**

2 1-30 **Listen and number.**

3 1-31 **Listen. Then ask and answer with a friend.**

4 1-32 **Play *Picture Bingo*. Listen and check (✓).**

28

5 Look and say with a friend. **?**

Story 2

1 Look at the pictures. What colors can you see?

Story 2

2 1-33 **Listen to the story. Find the kites from Activity 1.**

The Kite Festival

30

3 🎧 1-34 **Listen and check (✓).**

1

2

3

4

4 💬 **Draw your favorite kite. Tell a friend.**

Grammar 2

1  **BBC** **Watch Part 3 of the story video.** 2-4

Where's Dan?

2 🎧 1-35 **Listen and point. Then repeat.**

3 🎧 1-36 **Listen and number.**

4 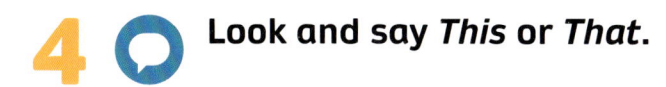 Look and say *This* or *That*.

1

2

3

Listening and Speaking 2

5 🎧 1-37 Listen and find. Then talk about the picture.

Phonics

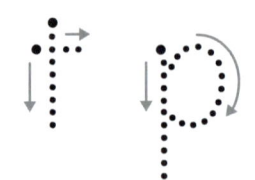

1 🎧 1-38   **Listen and repeat. Then trace.**

2 🎧 1-39   **Listen and check (✓) in red (t) or in green (p).**

3 💬 **Say the words. Check (✓) the odd one out.**

4 💡 **Think and say.**

Now I Know

1 1-40   **Listen and point. Then talk with a friend.**

2   **Choose a project.**

Draw a shape picture.

or

Design a kite.

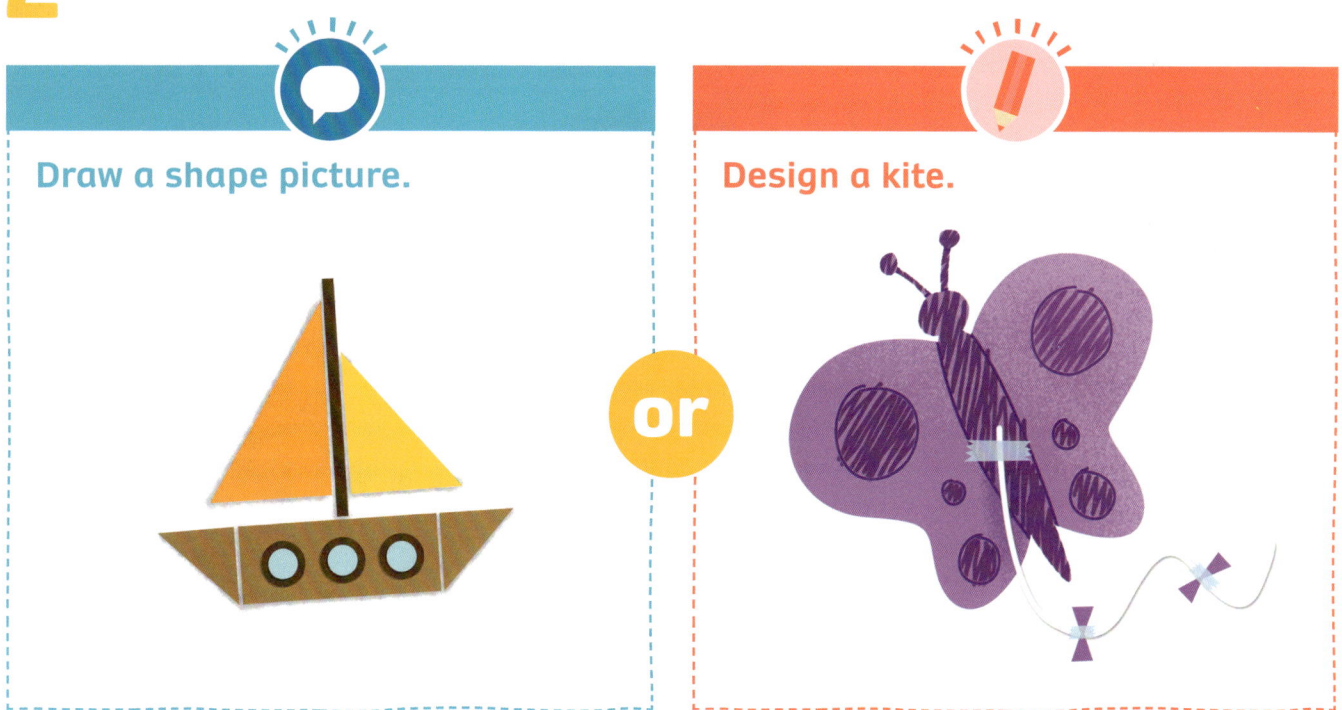

 **Color the stars**

 I can understand simple questions about things around me.

 I can name simple shapes and colors.

 3

What happens during the day?

Listening

- I can understand what people do every day.

Speaking

- I can say what I do every day.
- I can talk about different times of the day.

1 Check (✓) what you do before school.

2 Look at the picture. Draw your breakfast.

3  Watch the video. What do you do at night? Check (✓) or cross (X).

Vocabulary 1

1 1-41 Listen and repeat.

2 1-42 Listen and number.

3 1-43 Listen and say.

4 Match and say.

5 💬 Look and check (✓). Ask and answer.

 **?**

Story 1

1 💡 Think! What's in the story? Check (✓).

Story 1

2 🎧 1-44 Listen to the story. Check your answers from Activity 1.

3 🎧 1-45 Listen again and match.

1

a

b

2

c

3

d

4 When are they active? Check (✓).

1

2

3

5 💬 Talk with a friend. When are you active?

40

A Day in the Desert

1

2

Grammar 1

1  3-2  **Watch Part 1 of the story video. When does Tommy do his homework? Check (✓).**

2 1-46 **Listen and repeat.**

3  1-47 **Listen and number. Then say.**

42

4 **What do you do? Say in pairs.**

5 **Ask and answer with a friend.**

Listening

6 **1-48** **Listen and check (✓). Who's asking the questions?**

7 **1-49** **Listen again. Check (✓).**

Vocabulary 2

1 **Listen and repeat.**
1-50

2 **Listen and number.**
1-51

3 **Listen and say.**
1-52

4  **Say the activities in order.**

5  Match and say.

Story 2

1 Think about your day and draw!

2  1-53 Listen to the story. Check your answer from Activity 1.

My Perfect Day

3 🎧 **Listen again. Check (✓) or cross (✗).**

1-54

4 💬 **Talk about your perfect day.** ❓

Grammar 2

1   **Watch Part 2 of the story video. Check (✓).**

2 🎧 **Listen and repeat.**
1-55

3 💬 **Check (✓) or cross (X). Ask and answer with a friend.**

4   Listen and repeat.

5   Listen and match. Then ask and answer.

1	2	3	4

a	b	c	d

Speaking

6   Ask and answer with a friend.

7   Watch Part 3 of the story video. Who falls asleep?

Phonics

1 🎧 1-58 **Listen and repeat. Then trace.**

2 🎧 1-59 **Listen and check (✓) in red (i) or in blue (n). Then say.**

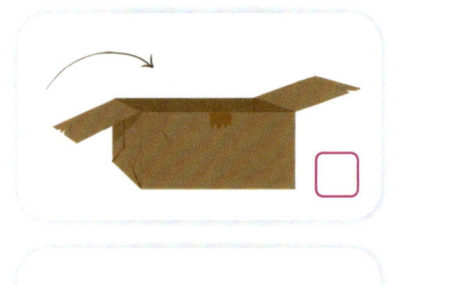

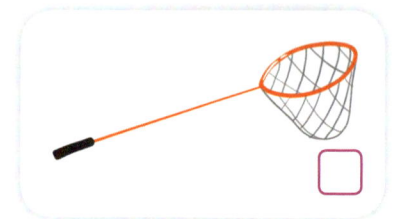

3 💬 **Say the words. Check (✓) the odd one out.**

1

2

3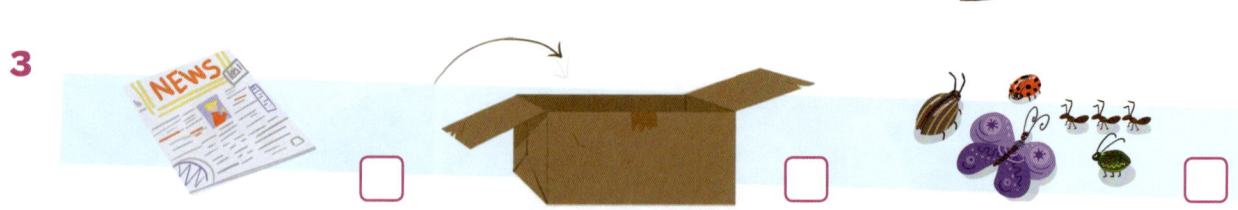

4 💬 **Draw and say.**

i   n

Now I Know

1  Talk about your favorite day. What do you do?

2 Choose a project.

Our activities

or

A schedule

Color the stars

 I can understand what people do every day.

 I can say what I do every day.

 I can talk about different times of the day.

Why do we have animals?

Listening

- I can understand questions about things around me.

Speaking

- I can talk about where things are.
- I can talk about animals I know.

1 💬 Say the animals in English.

1 3 5

2 4 6

2 💬 Look at the picture. What animals can you see?

3 ▶ 4-1 **BBC** Watch the video. Check (✓) the animals you hear.

Vocabulary 1

1 1-60 **Listen and repeat.**

goat ☐ sheep ☐ bee ☐ goose ☐

egg ☐ honey ☐ milk ☐ meat ☐

2 1-61 **Listen and number.**   **3** 1-62 **Listen and say.**

4 💬 **Check (✓) the odd one out. Say why.**

1

☐ ☐ ☐

2

☐ ☐ ☐

5 💡 **Think and match.** ❓

6 ▶ 4-1 **BBC** **Watch the video on animals again. Check your answers.**

Story 1

1 🎧 1-63 **Look at the pictures. Listen and point.**

Story 1

2 🎧 1-64 Listen to the story. Check your answers from Activity 1.

Amazing Animals

3 🎧 **Listen and check (✓).**

1-65

1

2

3

4

4 💬 **Talk with a friend. Do you use things that come from animals?** ❓

Grammar 1

1 4-2 **Watch Part 1 of the story video. Where are Tommy and Suzie?**

2 1-66 **Listen and repeat.**

1    2

3 **Look and say.**

1

3

2

4

4 Listen and check (✓).
1-67

1

3

2

4

Listening and Speaking

5  Listen and number.
1-68

6 Look at the picture. Ask and answer with a friend.

Vocabulary 2

1 1-69 **Listen and repeat.**

kitten ☐   puppy ☐   calf ☐   lamb ☐

kid ☐   duckling ☐   barn ☐   nest ☐

2 1-70 **Listen and number.**   **3** 1-71 **Listen and say.**

4 **Say the animal words.**

5 Listen and match.

6 Draw. Then talk with a friend.

Story 2

1 Look at the pictures. What's the story about?

Story 2

2 🎧 1-73 **Listen to the story. Check your answer from Activity 1.**

Cleo's Surprise!

3  1-74 **Listen and check (✓).**

4 **Draw and say.** ?

1

2

3

4

Grammar 2

1   **Watch Part 2 of the story video. Count the animals.**

4-3

2 🎧 **Listen and repeat.**

1-75

3 🎧 **Listen and check (✓) or cross (✗). Then say.**

1-76

4 Listen and match. Then say.

Speaking

5 Talk about the picture with a friend.

6  Watch Part 3 of the story video. What's wrong?

Phonics

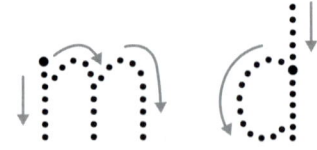

1 🎧 1-78 **Listen and repeat. Then trace.**

2 🎧 1-79 **Listen and check (✓) in blue (m) or in red (d). Then say.**

3 🎧 1-80 **Listen. Say the odd one out.**

4 💬 **Draw and say.**

m

d

Now I Know

1 Check (✓) or cross (✗).
Talk with a friend.

2 Choose a project.

Present your favorite farm animals.

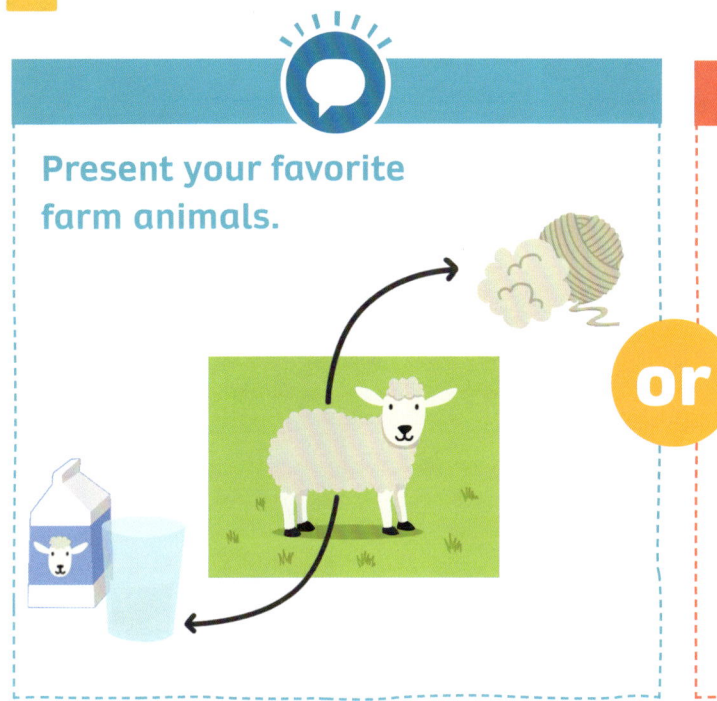

or

Make a poster about baby animals.

cow   duck

calf   duckling

★ ★ ★ ★ **Color the stars** ★ ★ ★ ★

 I can understand questions about things around me.

 I can talk about where things are.

 I can talk about animals I know.

5

What makes a family?

Listening

- I can understand information about families.

Speaking

- I can name my family members.
- I can ask and answer questions about my family and friends.

1

Who's in your family? Check (✓).

2

 **Look at the picture. Who can you see?**

3

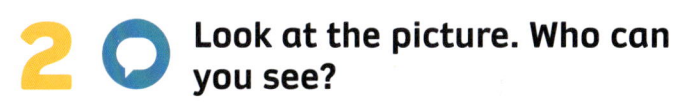 **Watch the video. Name the family members.**

5-1 BBC

1	2	3
		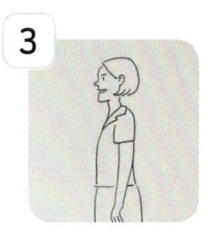

Vocabulary 1

1 🎧 1-81 **Listen and repeat.**

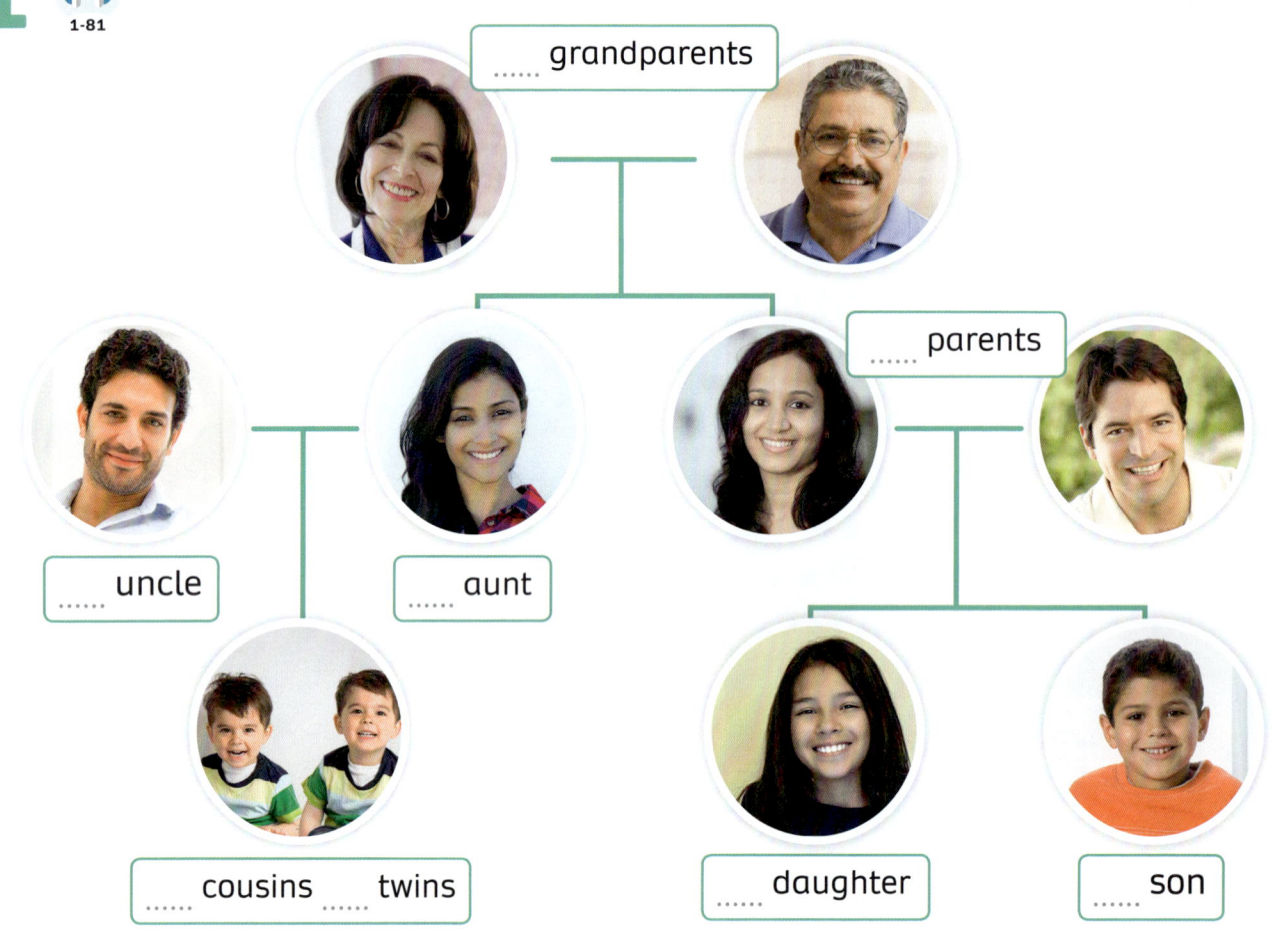

...... grandparents

...... parents

...... uncle

...... aunt

...... cousins   ...... twins

...... daughter

...... son

2 🎧 1-82 **Listen and number.**

3 🎧 1-83 **Listen and say. Who am I?**

4 🎧 1-84 **Listen and check (✓).**

5 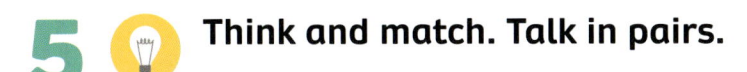 Think and match. Talk in pairs.

1 2 3 4

5 6 7 8

6 ▶ 5-1 BBC Watch the video again. Say the family members. ?

Story 1

1 🎧 1-85 Listen. What's the story about? Check (✓).

My Art Project

Story 1

2  1-86   **Listen to the story. Check your answer from Activity 1.**

3 1-87   **Listen and number.**

4  Find and color the frame. Then say.

   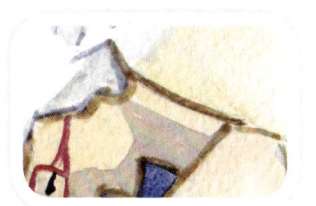

5 Talk in pairs. What's your favorite painting? Why?

Grammar 1

1   **Watch Part 1 of the story video. Who's the girl?**

5-2

2 **Listen and number.**

1-88

3   **Listen and repeat. Then talk in pairs.**

1-89

4 **Listen and check (✓).**

5 **Listen again and repeat.**

6  **Watch Part 2 of the story video. What happens to Miss Sparks?**

Speaking

7  **Listen. Draw three family members. Ask and answer.**

Vocabulary 2

1 2-01 **Listen and repeat.**

live together

talk

laugh

share

help

old

young

quiet

noisy

2 2-02 **Listen and number.**

3 2-03 **Listen and say.**

4  **Think about your family. Check (✓). Then tell a friend.**

5 **Think about your family. Draw.**

6  **Listen. Ask and answer.**
2-04

Story 2

1  **Listen. What's the story about? Check (✓).**
2-05

2 🎧 **Listen to the story. Check your answer from Activity 1.**

2-06

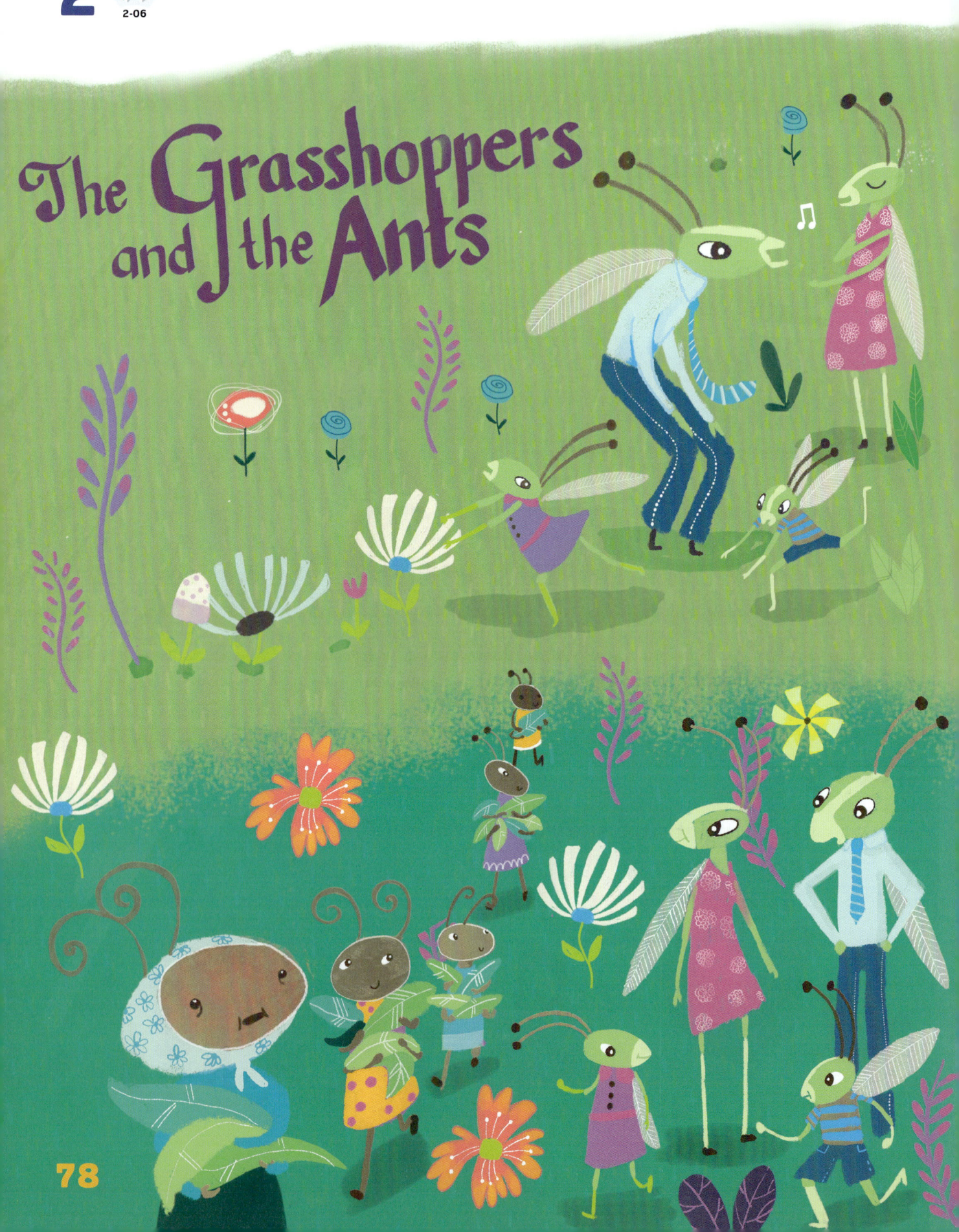

The Grasshoppers and the Ants

3 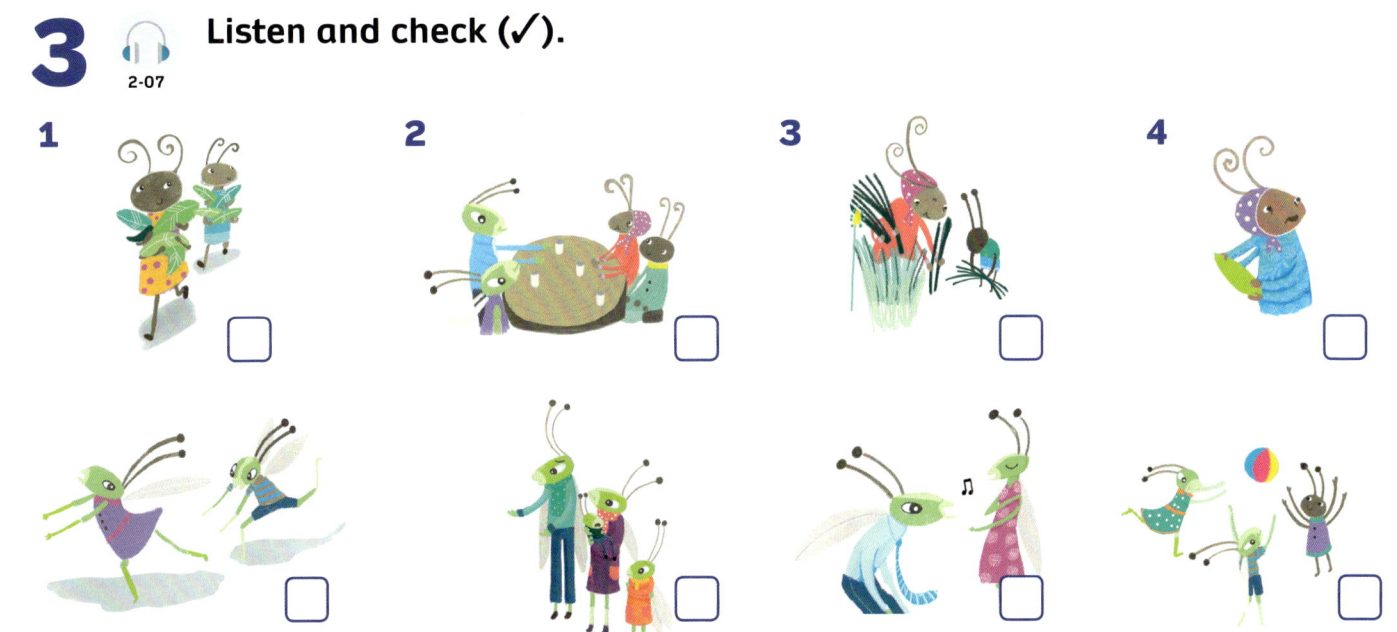 2-07 **Listen and check (✓).**

1

2

3

4

4 💡 **Think about the story. Talk in pairs.** ❓

Grammar 2

1   **Watch Part 3 of the story video. What do Tommy and Suzie do?**

2 🎧 **Listen and repeat.**
2-08

3 🎧 **Listen and number. Then say.**
2-09

4 💬 **Now talk about you and your family.**

5 Listen and repeat.
2-10

6 Who do you live with? Ask and answer.

Listening and Speaking

7 Listen and check (✓).
2-11

				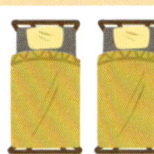		

8  Ask a friend about their family.

Phonics

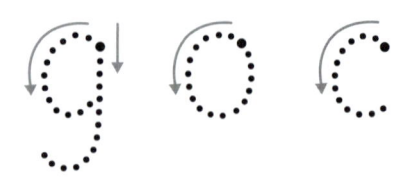

1 🎧 2-12 **Listen and repeat. Then trace.**

2 🎧 2-13 **Listen and number. Then match and say.**

a

b

c

3 🎧 2-14 **Listen. Color the words with *o*.**

4 💬 **Draw and say.**

g   o   c

5

Now I Know

1  **Think about you and your family. Check (✓) or cross (✗).**

2 **Choose a project.**

Family paintings.

or

A family tree.

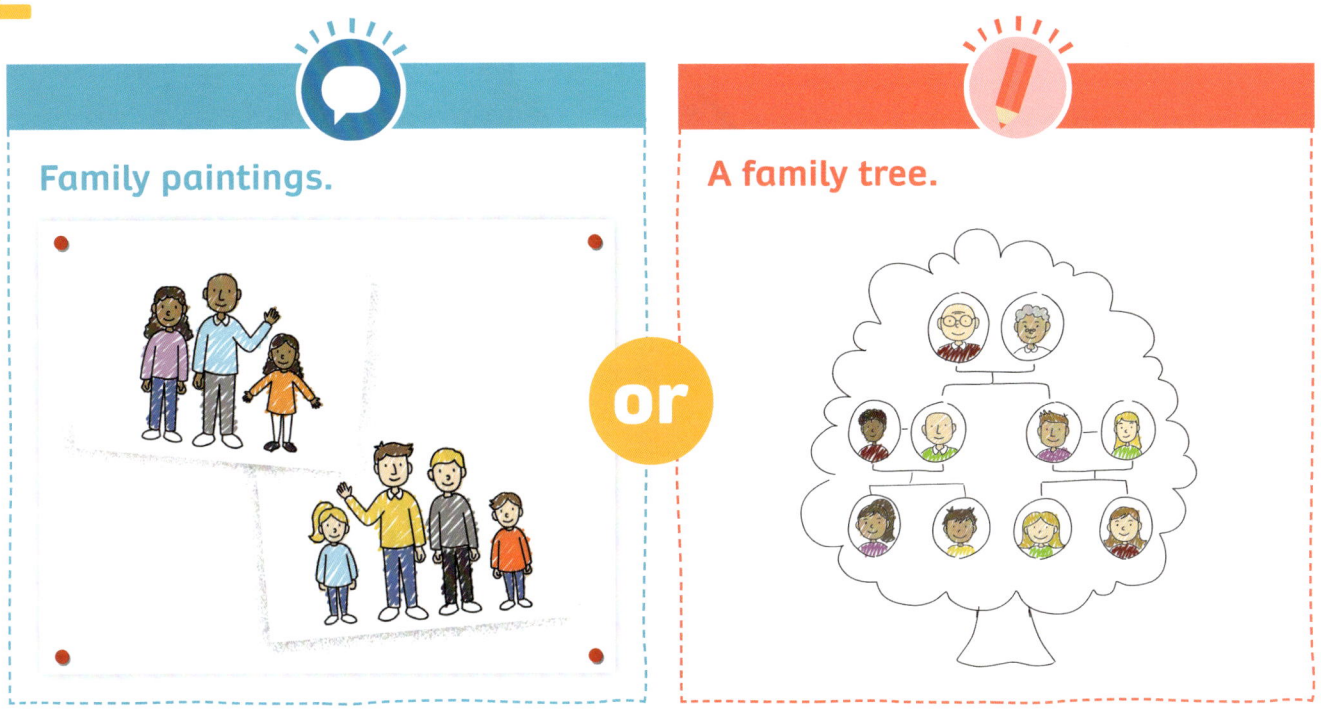

★ ★ ★ ★ **Color the stars** ★ ★ ★ ★

 I can understand information about families.

 I can name my family members.

 I can ask and answer questions about my family and friends.

6

How are we the same and different?

Listening

- I can understand what people look like.

Speaking

- I can talk about what someone looks like.
- I can give instructions for a dance.

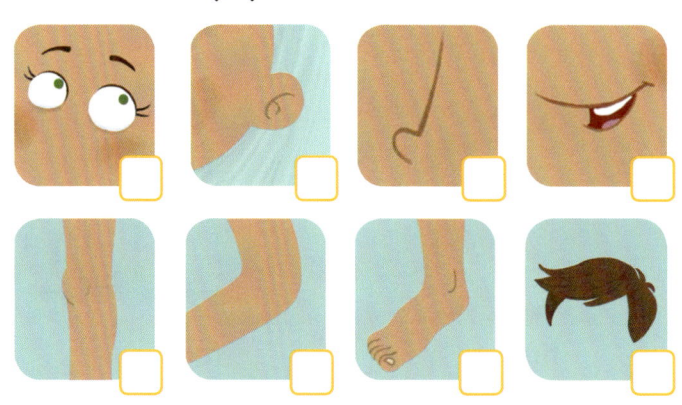

1 What body words do you know? Check (✓).

2 💬 Look at the picture. Say the body words.

3 ▶ 6-1 **BBC** Watch the video. Check (✓) the actions you see.

85

Vocabulary 1

1 **Listen and repeat.**

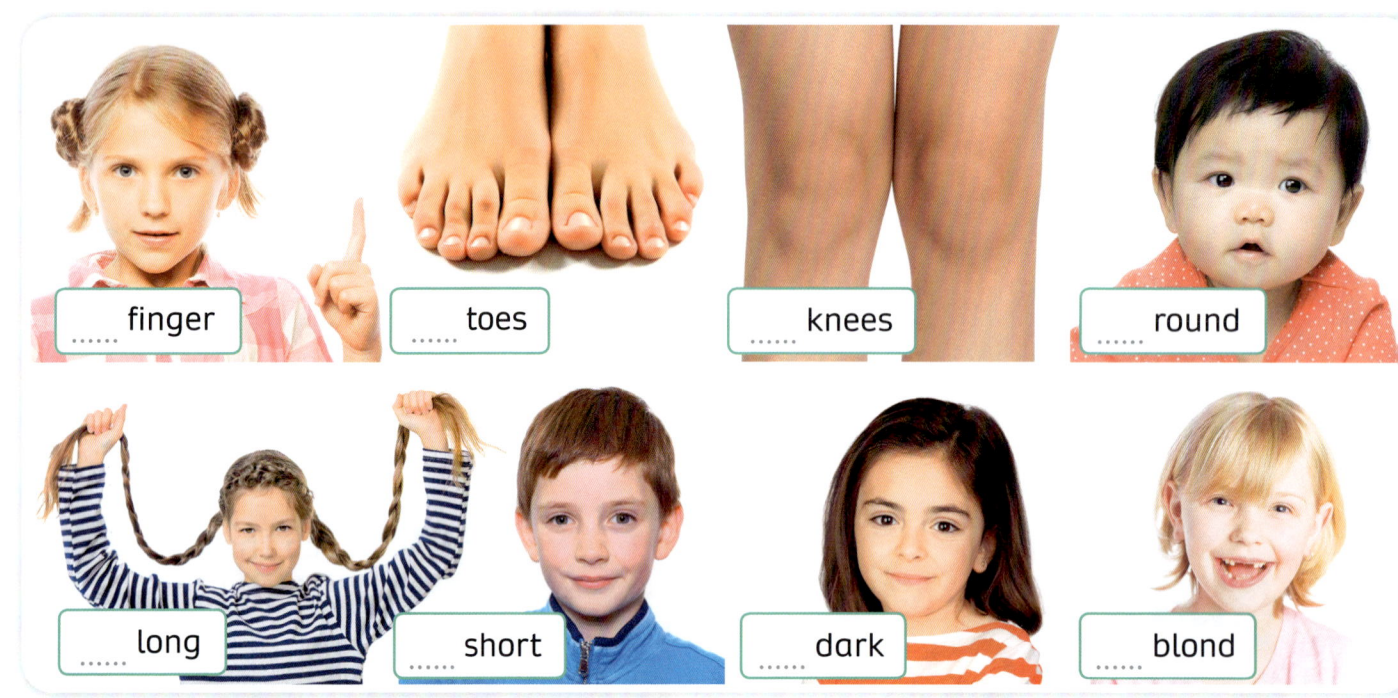

...... finger
...... toes
...... knees
...... round

...... long
...... short
...... dark
...... blond

2 **Listen and number.**

3 **Listen and say.**

4 **Listen and check (✓).**

5  **Draw and color. Then talk in pairs.**

6  **Tell the class about you and your friend.**

Story 1

1 **Look at the pictures. Describe the monsters.**

Story 1

2 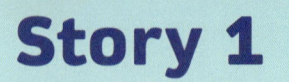 **2-19** Listen to the story. Check your answers from Activity 1.

1

A NEW MONSTER AT SCHOOL

2

6

4

3

3 2-20 Listen and check (✓).

1		
2		
3		
4		
5		

4 Draw a new monster. Tell a friend.

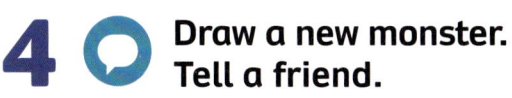

Grammar 1

1   **Watch Parts 1 and 2 of the story video. What body words do you hear?**

2 2-21 **Listen and number. Listen again and repeat.**

3 **Check (✓) or cross (✗). Who has dark hair?**

4 **Talk in pairs. Then tell the class.**

5 🎧 2-22 Listen and check (✓) or cross (✗).

1 ☐
2 ☐
3 ☐
4 ☐

6 🎧 2-23 Listen again and repeat. Ask and answer in pairs.

Speaking

7 💬 Complete for you. Ask two friends. Then tell the class.

Me				
....				
....				

Vocabulary 2

1 2-24 **Listen and repeat.**

dance

smile

bend

kick

snap

step

spin

wave

2 2-25 **Listen and number.**

3 2-26 **Listen and say. Do the actions.**

4 **Look and say.**

5 **Look and say. What can you do with … ?**

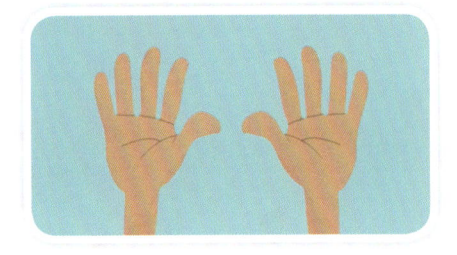 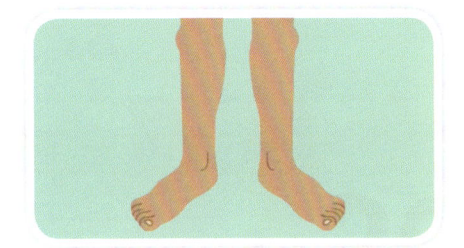 

6 2-27 **Listen and check (✓) or cross (✗).**

Story 2

1 2-28 **Listen and point.**

2 🎧 2-29 **Listen to the story. Check your answers from Activity 1.**

Dances Around The World

3 🎧 2-30 **Listen and check (✓).**

	1	2	3	4	5	6

4  Talk in pairs. Describe your favorite dance.

Grammar 2

1  6-3 **Watch Part 3 of the story video. Do the actions.**

2 2-31 **Listen and check (✓) or cross (✗). Listen again and repeat.**

1　　　2　　　3　　　4

3 2-32 **Listen and number. Then say.**

4
2-33
Listen and repeat. Then talk about your friends.

5
2-34
Listen and match. Then say.

Listening and Speaking

6
2-35
Listen and check (✓). Listen again and do the dance.

7
Work in pairs. Invent a dance.

Phonics

1 🎧 2-36 **Listen and repeat. Then trace.**

2 🎧 2-37 **Listen and check (✓) the words with *c* or *k*. Then say.**

3 🎧 2-38 **Listen and color. Then say.**

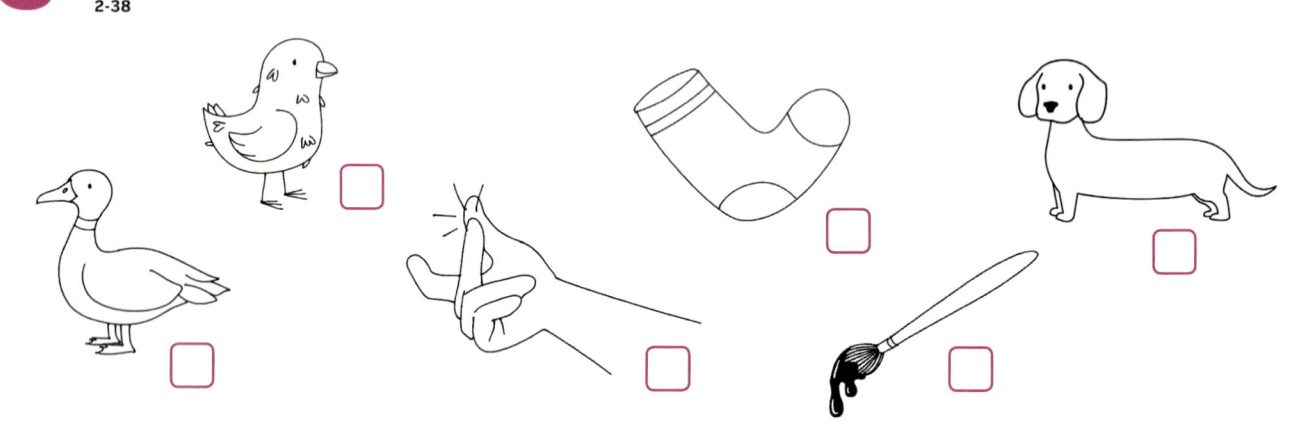

4 💬 **Draw and say.**

98

Now I Know

1  **Think about you and your family. Look and say.**

   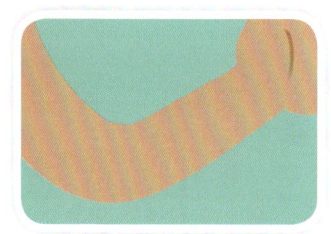

2 **Choose a project.**

A dance presentation. | **or** | A passport.

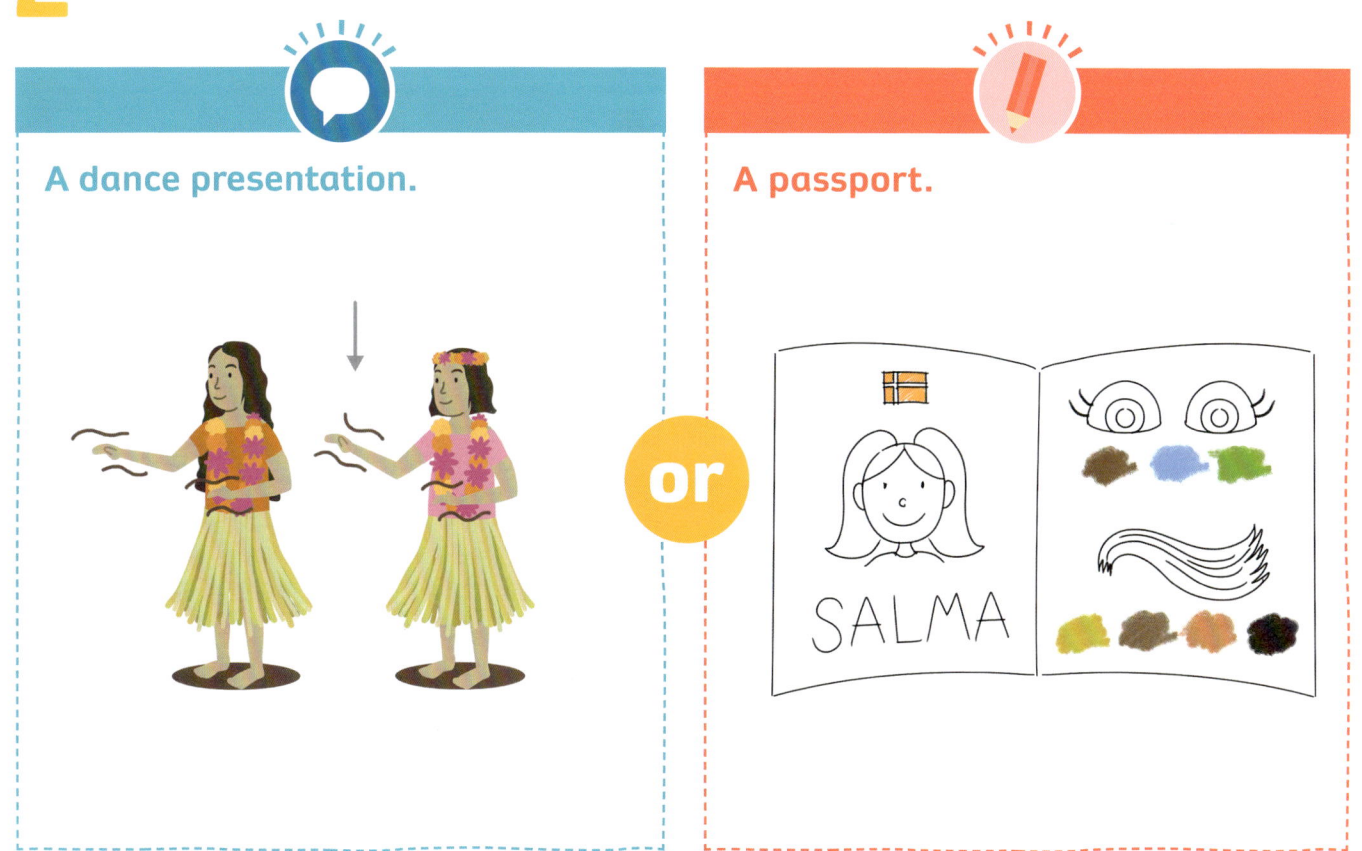

★ ★ ★ ★ Color the stars ★ ★ ★ ★

 I can understand what people look like.

 I can talk about what someone looks like.

 I can give instructions for a dance.

Why do we do hobbies?

Listening

- I can understand what people can and can't do.

Reading

- I can read simple words.

Speaking

- I can give instructions in a game.
- I can say what I can and can't do.

Writing

- I can copy simple words.

1 What do you use to ride a bike? Circle.

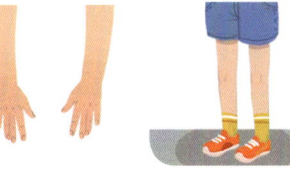  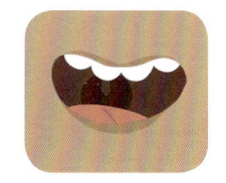

arms   legs   head   mouth

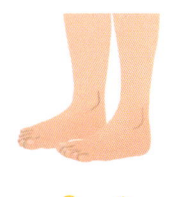  

feet   ears   eyes

2 Look at the picture. Talk in pairs.

3 7-1 **BBC** Watch the video and check (✓).

4 7-1 **BBC** Watch the video again. Do the actions.

Vocabulary 1

1 **Listen and repeat.**
2-39

...... skip ...... hop ...... swim ...... ride a bike

...... take pictures ...... climb ...... type ...... code

2 **Listen and number.**
2-40

3 **Listen and say.**
2-41

4 **Trace and match.**

 a

 c

b

1 skip

2 climb

3 swim

4 ride a bike

5 code

6 hop

 d

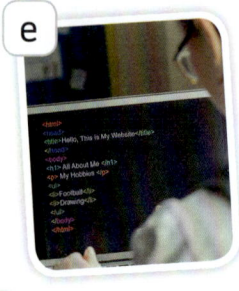 e

 f

5 Use the words in Activity 1. Write for you.

6  **7-1**  Watch the video again. Check (✓).

Story 1

1 Look and say. What can they do?

Story 1

2 2-42   Listen to the story. Check your answer from Activity 1.

THE GREENS AND THE HOMES

104

3 Listen again. Check (✓) the actions you hear.
2-43

4 Listen and say *The Greens* or *The Homes.*
2-44

5 What do you do with your family? Say.

Grammar 1

1  **BBC** Watch Parts 1 and 2 of the story video. Can Cranky swim?

2 Listen and repeat.

> **Grammar**
>
> I **can** swim
> I **can't** swim.
>
> **Can** you swim?
> **Yes**, I **can**./**No**, I **can't**.

3 Listen and number.

4 Tell a friend. Use *I can … / I can't … .*

5 Ask and answer in pairs.

6 Think of your family and say.

Listening and Speaking

7 🎧 2-47 Listen and check (✓) or cross (✗).

	bike	type fast	hop x10	swim	climb	play soccer
Emma						
My friend						

8 Ask and answer with a friend.

Can you type fast?

No, I can't.

Vocabulary 2

1 2-48 **Listen and repeat.**

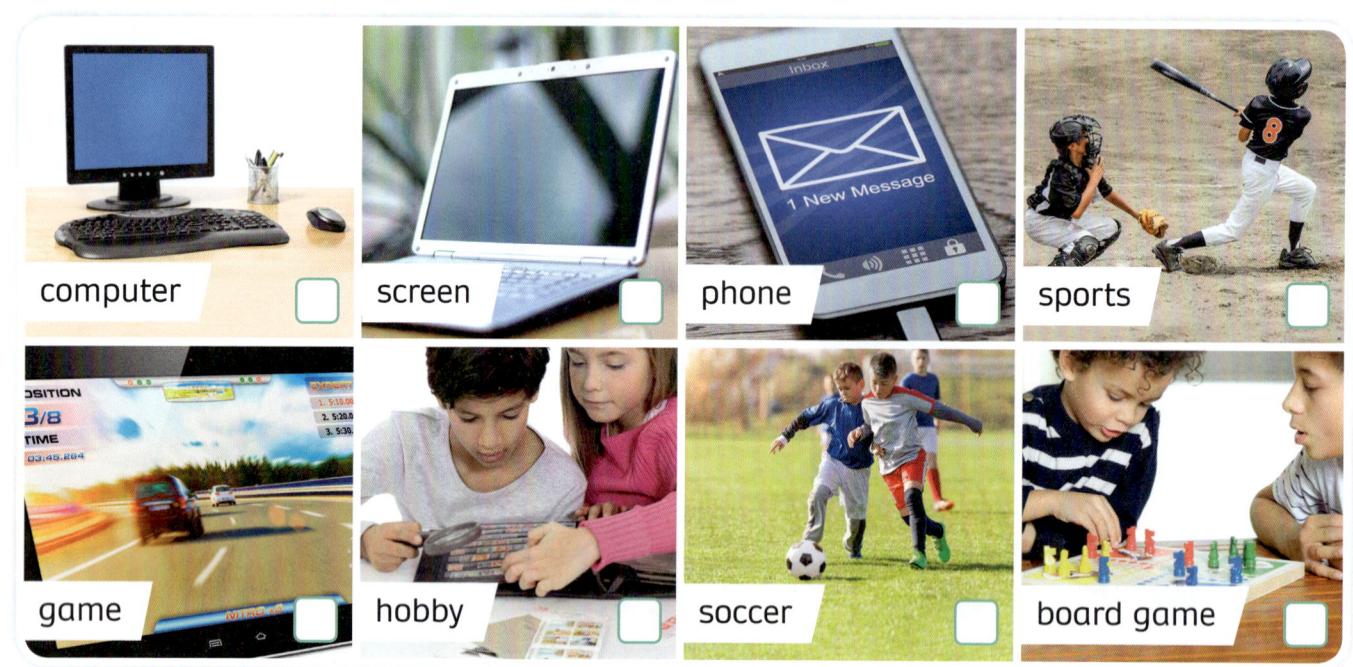

computer

screen

phone

sports

game

hobby

soccer

board game

2 2-49 **Listen and check (✓). Use different colors.**

3 2-50 **Listen and say.**

4 **Look at the photos and trace.**

1

game

3

phone

2

hobby

4

soccer

5 **Read and draw.**

Hobby	Board game
Sports	Game

6  **Listen. Then ask and answer.**
2-51

Story 2

1 **What can you do at the Olympics or Paralympics? Check (✓).**

Story 2

2 🎧 2-52 Listen. Check your answers from Activity 1.

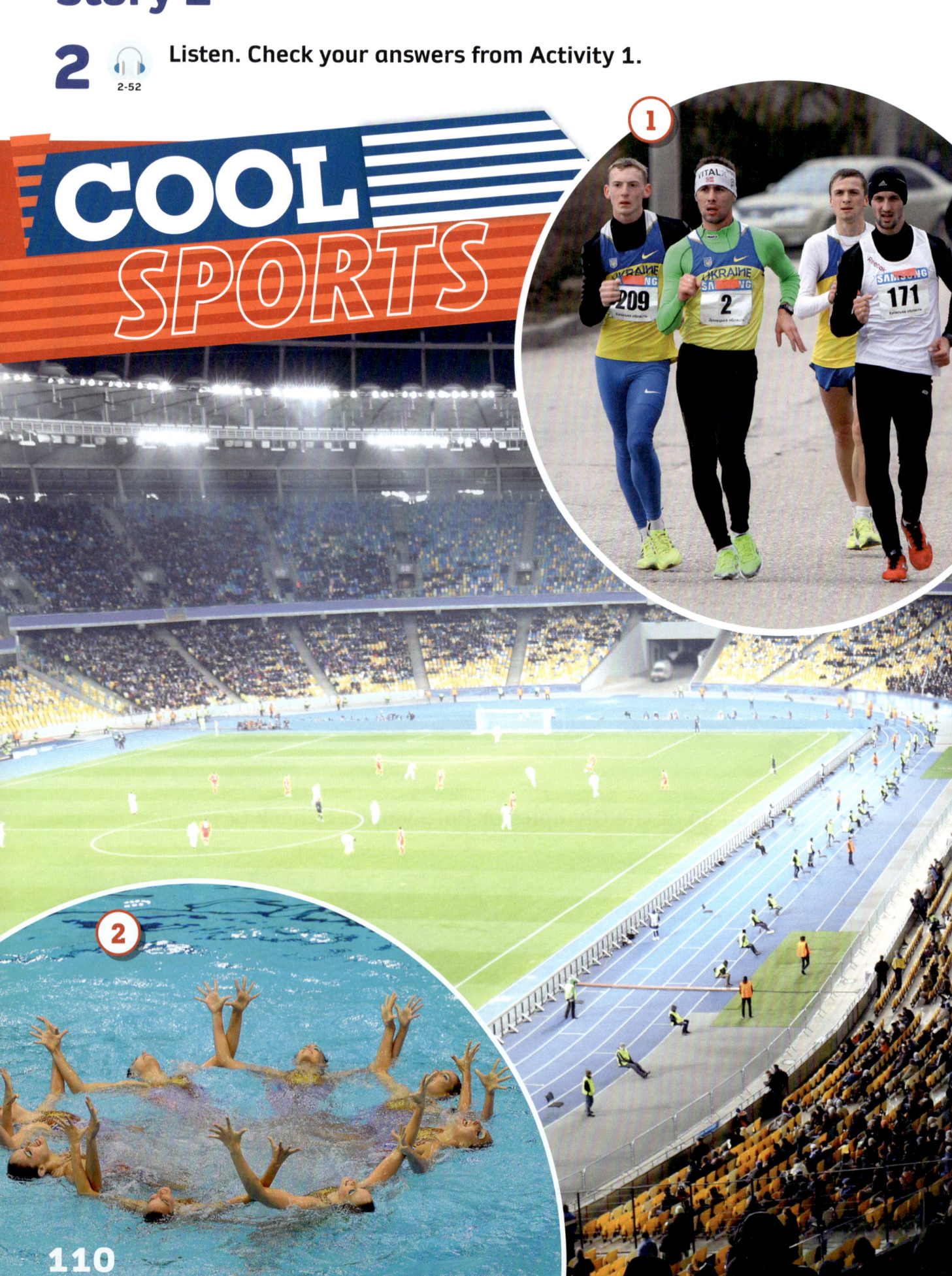

COOL SPORTS

3 Look at the pictures. Think and check (✓).

1					
2					
3					
4					
5					

4 Talk in pairs. What Olympic sports can you do?

Grammar 2

1  **BBC** **Watch Part 2 of the story video again. What does Suzie say?**

Look at me!

2 🎧 2-53 **Listen and repeat.**

Grammar

I	me
you	you
he	him
she	her
we	us
they	them

3 2-54 **Listen and say.**

1

3

2

4

4 **Listen and follow. Draw. Then play!**

2-55

Speaking

5 **Listen and number. Then play.**

2-56

6   **Watch Part 3 of the story video. Can Dan sing?**

7-3

Phonics

r u b

1 🎧 2-57 **Listen and repeat. Then trace.**

2 🎧 2-58 **Listen and check (✓). Then say.**

u

r

b

3 🎧 2-59 **Listen and color. Then say.**

4 💬 **Draw and say.**

r

u

r

b

Now I Know

1 **Draw and say.**

I can ... ✔

I can't ... ✖

2 **Talk to a friend. What are your hobbies?**

Talk about an athlete.

RUNNER

or

3 Choose a project.

 A hobby club.

SOCCER CLUB

Color the stars

 I can understand what people can and can't do.

 I can give instructions in a game. I can say what I can and can't do.

 I can read simple words.

 I can copy simple words.

8

What food do we eat?

Listening
- I can understand what others like and don't like.

Reading
- I can read simple words.

Speaking
- I can say what I like and don't like.

Writing
- I can copy simple words.

1 What food words do you know? Circle.

apple   orange   banana

meat   milk   egg

fish   chicken

2  Look at the picture. Talk in pairs.

3 ▶ 8-1 BBC Watch the video and check (✓). What do the children do?

 ☐    ☐    ☐

Vocabulary 1

1 🎧 2-60 **Listen and repeat.**

...... pineapple

...... grapes

...... pear

...... lemon

...... carrot

...... onion

...... potato

...... peas

2 🎧 2-61 **Listen and number.**

3 🎧 2-62 **Listen and say.**

4 **Read and match.**

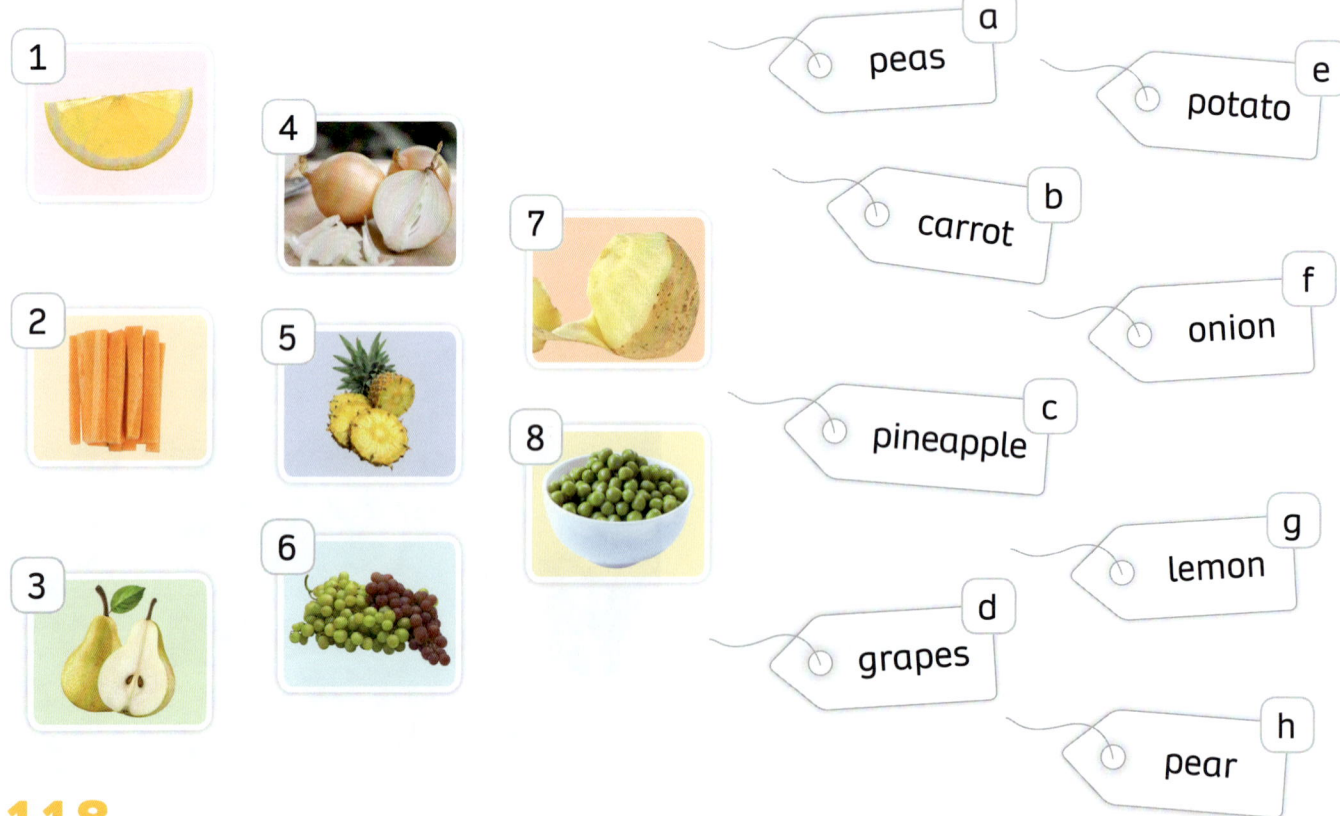

1

2

3

4

5

6

7

8

a peas

b carrot

c pineapple

d grapes

e potato

f onion

g lemon

h pear

5 Write the food words.

carrot   grapes   lemon   onion   peas
pear   pineapple   potato

Fruit

....

....

....

....

Vegetable

....

....

....

....

Story 1

1 Look at the pictures. What's the story about? Check (✓).

Story 1

2 🎧 2-63 **Listen. Check your answer from Activity 1.**

3 🎧 2-64 **Listen and check (✓).**

1

2

3

4

5

4 💬 **Talk with a friend. What's your favorite food art?** ❓

5 💬 **Draw your own food art. Then tell a friend.**

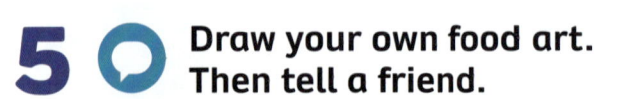

120

Food Art!

Fruit peacock!

Tangerine fish!

Your food art!

Grammar 1

1  **Watch Part 1 of the story video. Say three food words you hear.**

8-2

2  **Listen. Read and repeat.**

2-65

Grammar

I **like** bananas. ✅   **Do** you **like** bananas? 🍌❓

I **don't like** oranges. 🍊❌   **Yes**, I **do**. ✅ / **No**, I **don't**. ❌

3 **Listen and match.**

2-66

a    b    c    d    e    f

   🙂    😐

4 **Say for you. Tell the class.**

5   **Listen and check (✓) or cross (✗).**

Speaking

6 **Complete for you. Then ask two friends.**

	potatoes	grapes	peas	pears	carrots	onions
Me						
....						
....						

Do you like grapes?

Do you like onions?

Yes, I do.

No, I don't.

Vocabulary 2

1 2-68 **Listen and repeat.**

bread · rice · beans · pasta

lime · cookies · yogurt · soup

2 2-69 **Listen and number.**

3 2-70 **Listen and say.**

4 **Look and trace.**

1 lime

3 rice

5 beans

2 yogurt

4 cookies

6 soup

5 **Listen. Then write words from Activity 1.**

2-71

1

2

3

4

5

Story 2

1 **Look at the pictures. What's the story about? Check (✓).**

Story 2

2 🎧 2-72 Listen to the story. Check your answer from Activity 1.

The Fox and the Stork

126

8

3 🎧 2-73 **Listen again. What's in the soups? Check (✓).**

4 🎧 2-74 **Listen and check (✓) or cross (✗).**

1
2

3
4

5 💡 **Think about the story. Talk in pairs.**

Grammar 2

1   8-3 **Watch Part 2 of the story video. Does Cranky like blue food?**

2 2-75 **Listen. Read and repeat.**

Grammar

 He like**s** blue peas.

 Does he like blue peas?

 Does she like blue peas?

 She **doesn't** like blue peas.

Yes, he **does**.

No, she **doesn't**.

3 2-76 **Listen and match.**

a    b    c    d    e

4 **Look at Activity 3. Say what Cranky likes/doesn't like.**

128

5   Listen and answer.

Listening and Speaking

6   Listen. Who is it?

7   Ask and answer with a friend.

	 		 	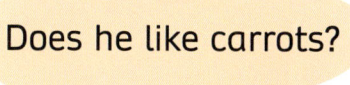	
 Sam	✓	✗	✓	✓	✗
 Lisa	✗	✓	✓	✗	✗
 James	✓	✗	✗	✗	✓
 Anna	✓	✗	✓	✓	✗

Does he like carrots?

No, he doesn't.

Is it James?

Yes!

8   Watch Part 3 of the story video. Does Cranky like picnics?

Phonics

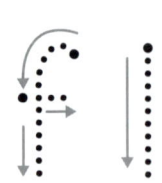

1 🎧 2-79 **Listen and repeat. Then trace.**

2 🎧 2-80 **Listen and check (✓) or cross (✗). Then say the words.**

3 🎧 2-81 **Listen and color. Then say.**

4 🎧 2-82 **Listen and trace. Then check (✓).**

130

8

Now I Know

1
2-83
Listen and draw. Then talk in pairs.

2 **Choose a project.**

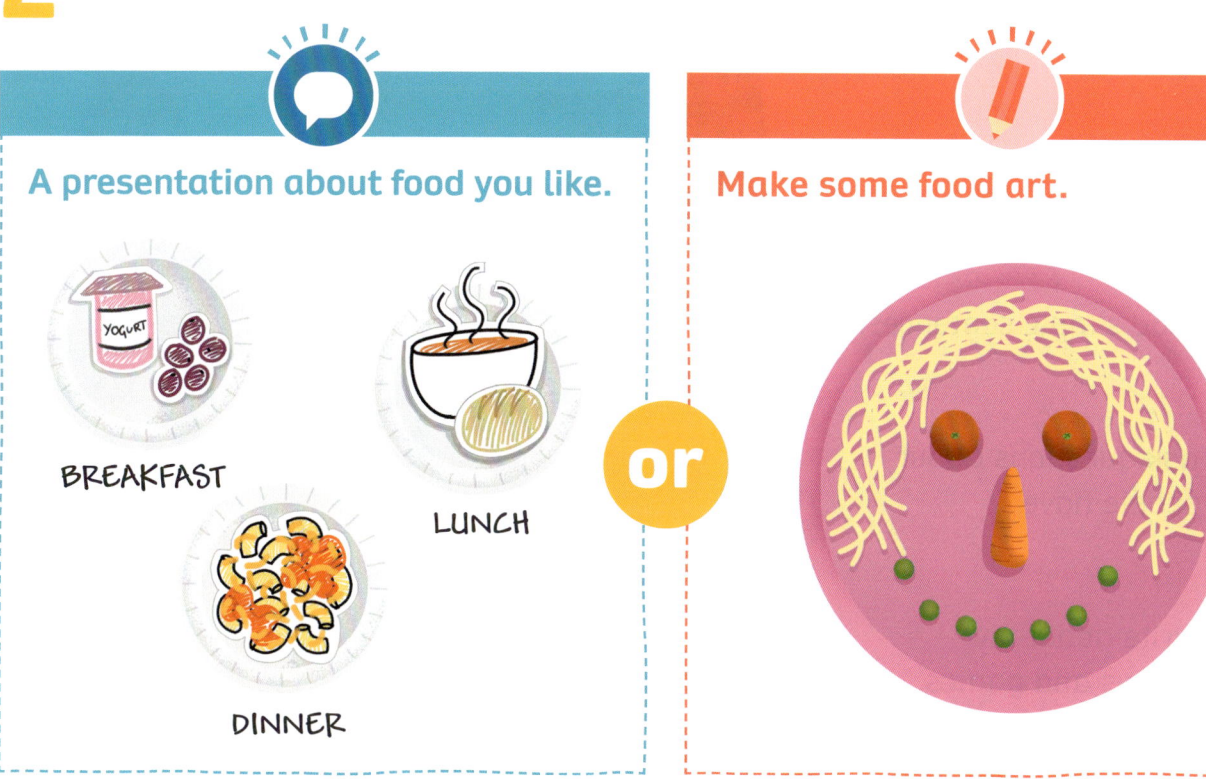

A presentation about food you like.

BREAKFAST

LUNCH

DINNER

or

Make some food art.

Color the stars

 I can understand what others like and don't like.

 I can say what I like and don't like.

 I can read simple words.

 I can copy simple words.

9

How do we play?

Listening
- I can understand what people have.

Reading
- I can read simple sentences.

Speaking
- I can ask questions about what people have.

Writing
- I can write about my favorite toys and games.

1 💬 What toys do you like playing with? Tell a friend.

> I like playing with cars.

2 💬 Look at the picture. Talk in pairs.

3 💬 Look at the picture. What toys do you have? Tell a friend.

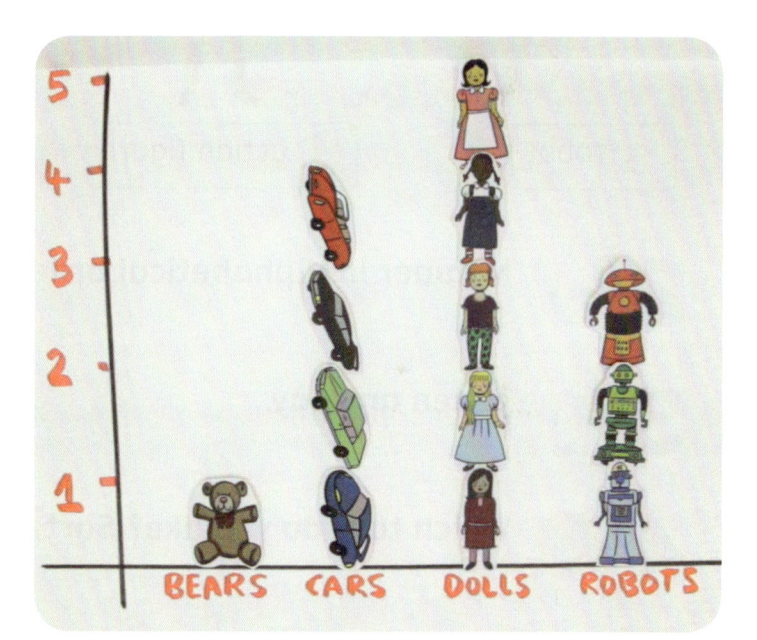

5
4
3
2
1

BEARS   CARS   DOLLS   ROBOTS

4 ▶ 9-1 **BBC** Watch the video and check (✓). How many children like cars?

| one | ☐ | three | ☐ |
| two | ☐ | four | ☐ |

Vocabulary 1

1 2-84 **Listen and repeat.**

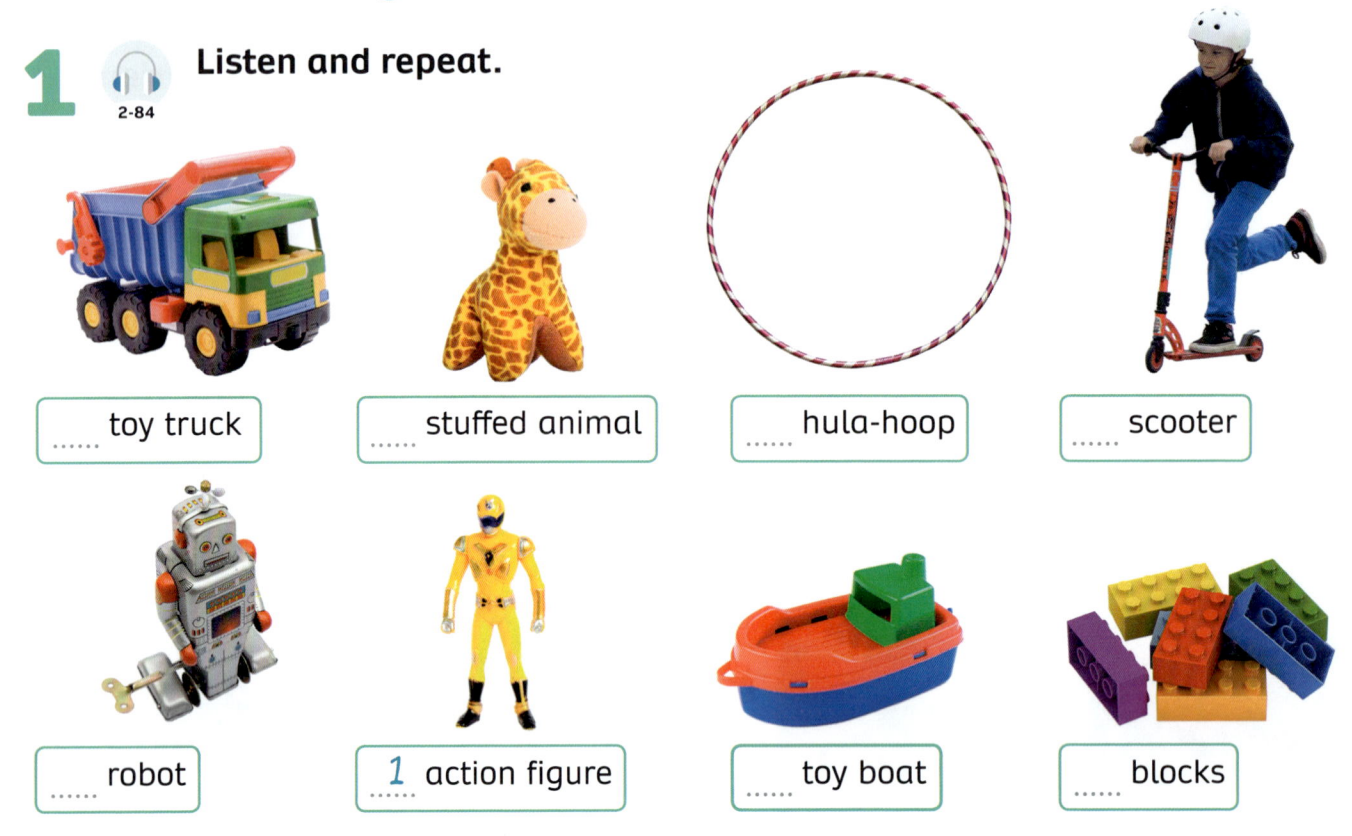

| ...... toy truck | ...... stuffed animal | ...... hula-hoop | ...... scooter |
| ...... robot | *1* action figure | ...... toy boat | ...... blocks |

2 2-85 **Number in alphabetical order. Then listen and check.**

3 2-86 **Listen and say.**

4 **Which toys do you like? Sort.**

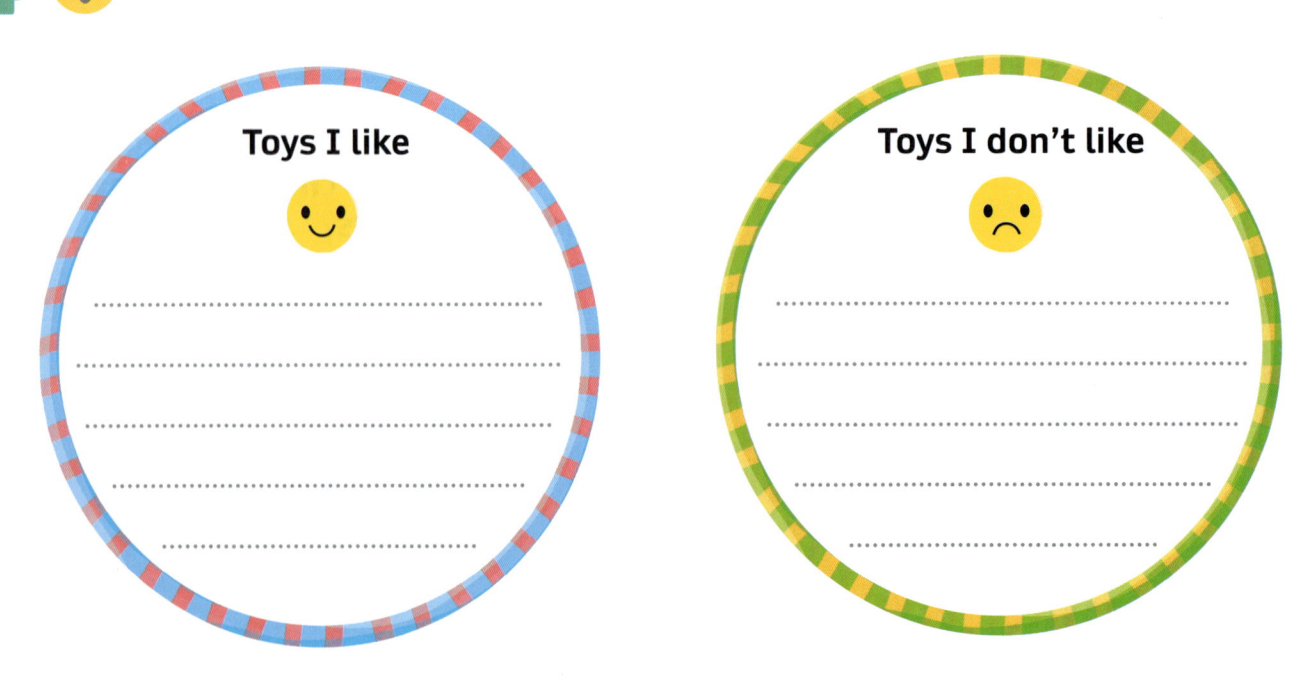

Toys I like 😊

Toys I don't like 🙁

5  **Watch the video again. Do a survey.**

9-1

What's your favorite toy?

My robot.

6 **What's your favorite playground game? Trace and write.**

My favorite
playground
game is

Story 1

1 **Look at the pictures. Who do you think they are? Check (✓).**

☐ brothers and sisters   ☐ cousins   ☐ friends

Story 1

2 2-87   Listen to the story. Check your answer from Activity 1.

3  **Listen and number.**

3-01

4  **Talk with a friend. What games do you play with your friends? Do you like to share your toys? Why?/Why not?**

Grammar 1

1  **BBC** 9-2 **Watch Parts 1 and 2 of the story video. Whose robot is it? Check (✓).**

2 3-02 **Look at the grammar box. Listen. Read and repeat.**

Grammar

Whose doll is this?

Whose robot is this?

It's Suzie**'s** doll.

It's Tommy**'s** robot.

3 **Read and match.**

1. It's Mom's computer.

2. This is Hugo's bike.

3. This is Dad's cell phone.

4. It's Carrie's hula-hoop.

4 Look and write.

 Jill  Nick

1 Whose monster is this?

It's .... monster.

2 .... teddy bear is this?

It's .... teddy bear.

Listening and Speaking 1

5 **3-03** Listen and match.

Adriana

Josh

Gina

Rashad

6 Play a game in groups.

Whose car is this?

It's Pedro's car.

Vocabulary 2

1   **Listen and repeat.**
3-04

win • lose • swings • slide

monkey bars • hopscotch • tag • take turns

2 **Listen and check (✓).**
3-05 **Use different colors.**

3 **Listen and say.**
3-06

4 **How do you play? Match and write.**

   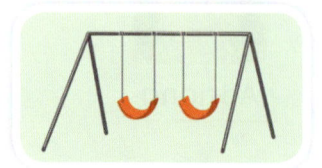

 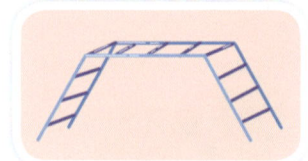  

Things in the playground	Playground games	How to play

5 🎧 3-07 Trace. Listen and match.

1

2

3

lose

win

take turns

a

b

c

Story 2

1 💡 Look at the title. Who do you think is in the text? Check (✓).

Playground Games

1

2

3

Story 2

2 🎧 3-08 Listen to the story. Check your answers from Activity 1.

Playground Games

CHILE

3 🎧 3-09 Listen and check (✓).

		1	2	3	4	5
CHILE						
INDIA						
JAPAN						

INDIA

JAPAN

4 **Think about the games in the story. Talk in pairs.**

Grammar 2

1  9-3 **BBC** **Watch Part 2 of the story video again. Are the toys Cranky's?**

It's mine.

2 3-10 **Look at the grammar box. Listen and match.**

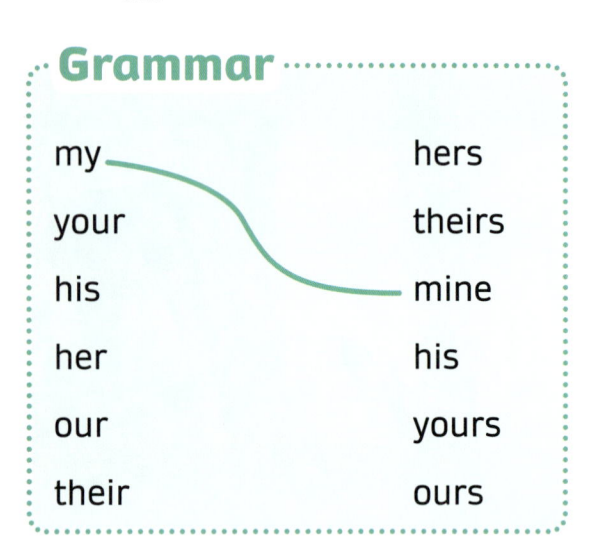

> ## Grammar
>
> | my | hers |
> |------|--------|
> | your | theirs |
> | his | mine |
> | her | his |
> | our | yours |
> | their | ours |

3 **Follow the lines and say for Lua.**

The robot is hers.

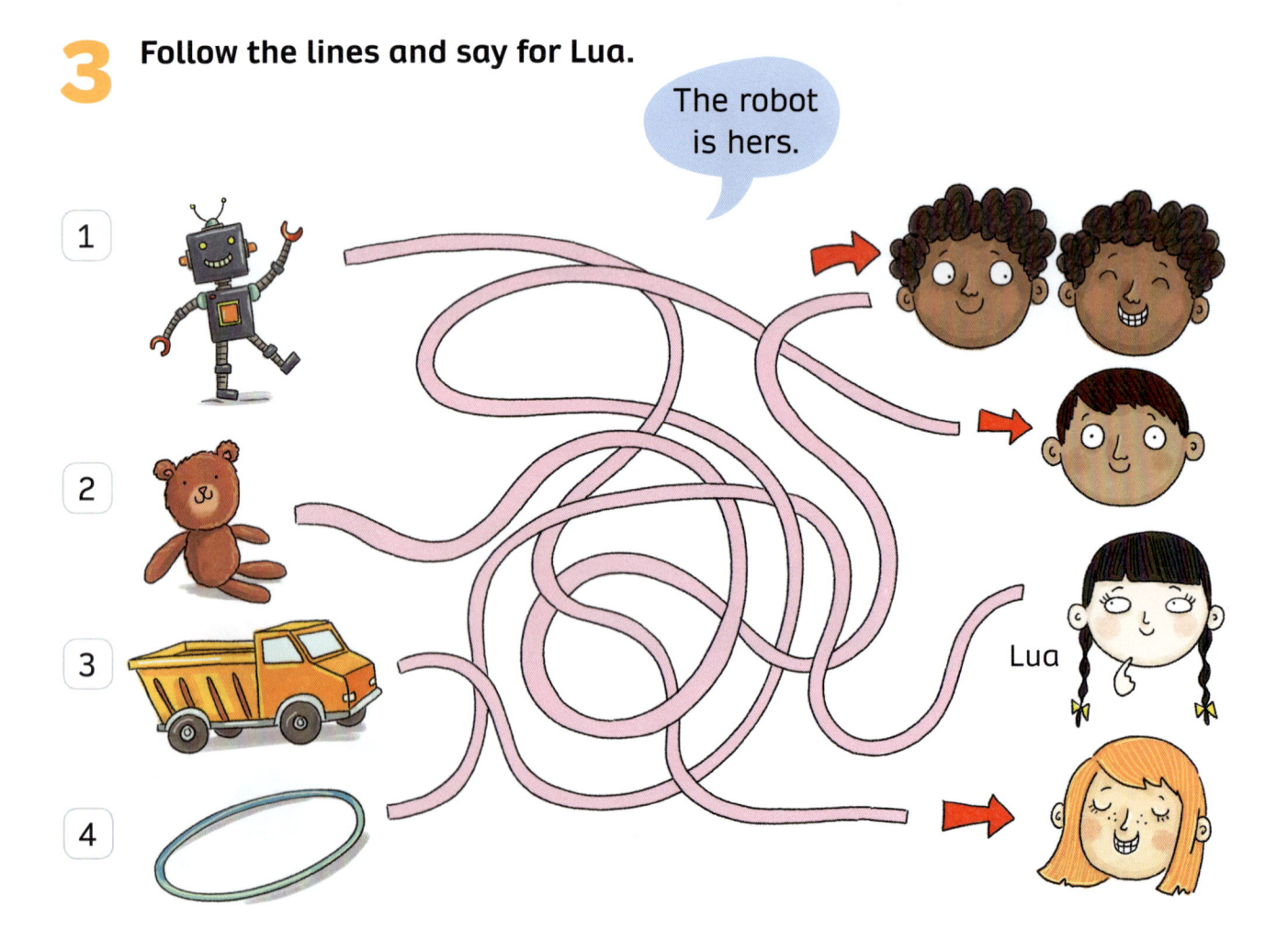

1

2

3

4

Lua

144

4 Look, read, and complete.

1. This tablet is ....

2. This action figure is ....

3. That cat is ....

Listening and Speaking 2

5 Draw yourself. Then listen and check (✓).

3-11

1

2

3

6 Play a game in groups.

Is this yours?

I think this is hers.

7 BBC Watch Part 3 of the story video. Does Cranky like sharing?

9-4

Phonics

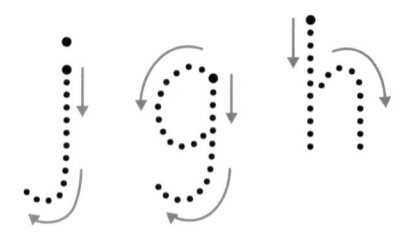

1 🎧 3-12 **Listen and repeat. Then trace.**

2 🎧 3-13 **Listen and match. Then say the words.**

j g h

3 🎧 3-14 **Listen and check (✓) the odd one out.**

4 **Draw and write.**

g   j   h

....

Now I Know

1 How do we play? Think and write.

- My favorite toys are .... , ... , and ....
- I play .... with my friends.

2 Choose a project.

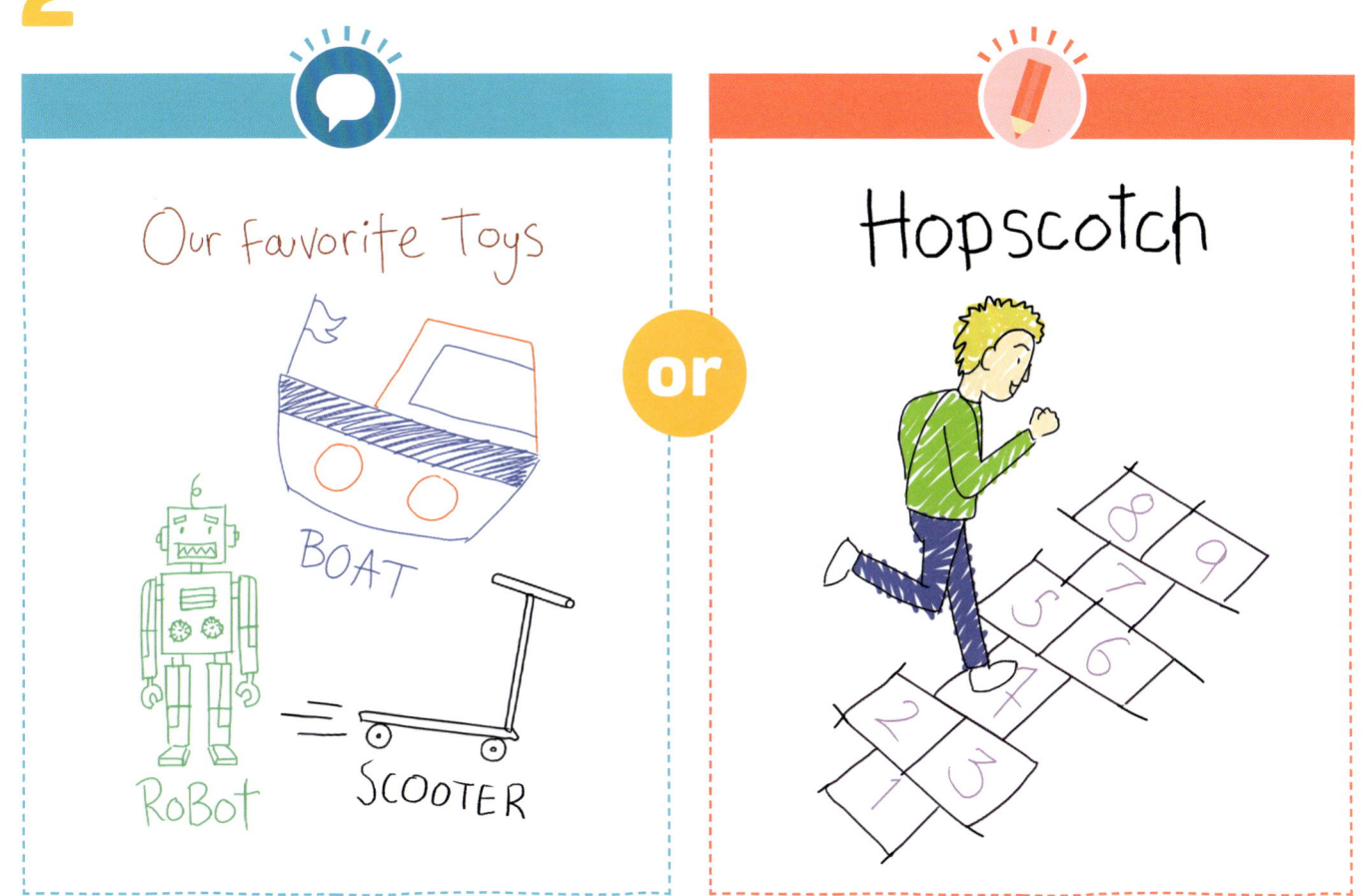

Our Favorite Toys

BOAT

ROBOT   SCOOTER

or

Hopscotch

Color the stars

 I can understand what people have.

 I can ask questions about what people have.

 I can read simple sentences.

 I can write about my favorite toys and games.

10

What clothes do we wear?

Listening
- I can identify someone from a description.

Reading
- I can read new words in short, simple sentences.

Speaking
- I can talk about what people are wearing.

Writing
- I can write simple clothes words.

1 What clothes words do you know? Circle.

 **shirt**  **T-shirt**  **jeans**  **pants**

skirt **dress** **shoes** **socks**

2 Look at the picture. What clothes can you see?

3 10-1  Watch the video. Say the clothes words you hear.

4 Choose a sport. Draw the clothes.

Vocabulary 1

1 **Listen and repeat.**
3-15

.... sweater

.... blouse

.... jacket

.... shorts

.... boots

.... sandals

.... gloves

.... bathing suit

2 **Listen and number.**
3-16

3 **Listen and say.**
3-17

4 **Read and circle.**

I'm wearing …

1   … **a bathing suit / a sweater**.

3   … **boots / gloves**.

2   … **shorts / a blouse**.

4   … **a jacket / sandals**.

5 **Write. Use the words from Activity 1.**

What clothes are good ...

... for sports?

... in the summer?

... in the winter?

Story 1

1 **What are the clothes made from? Match and say.**

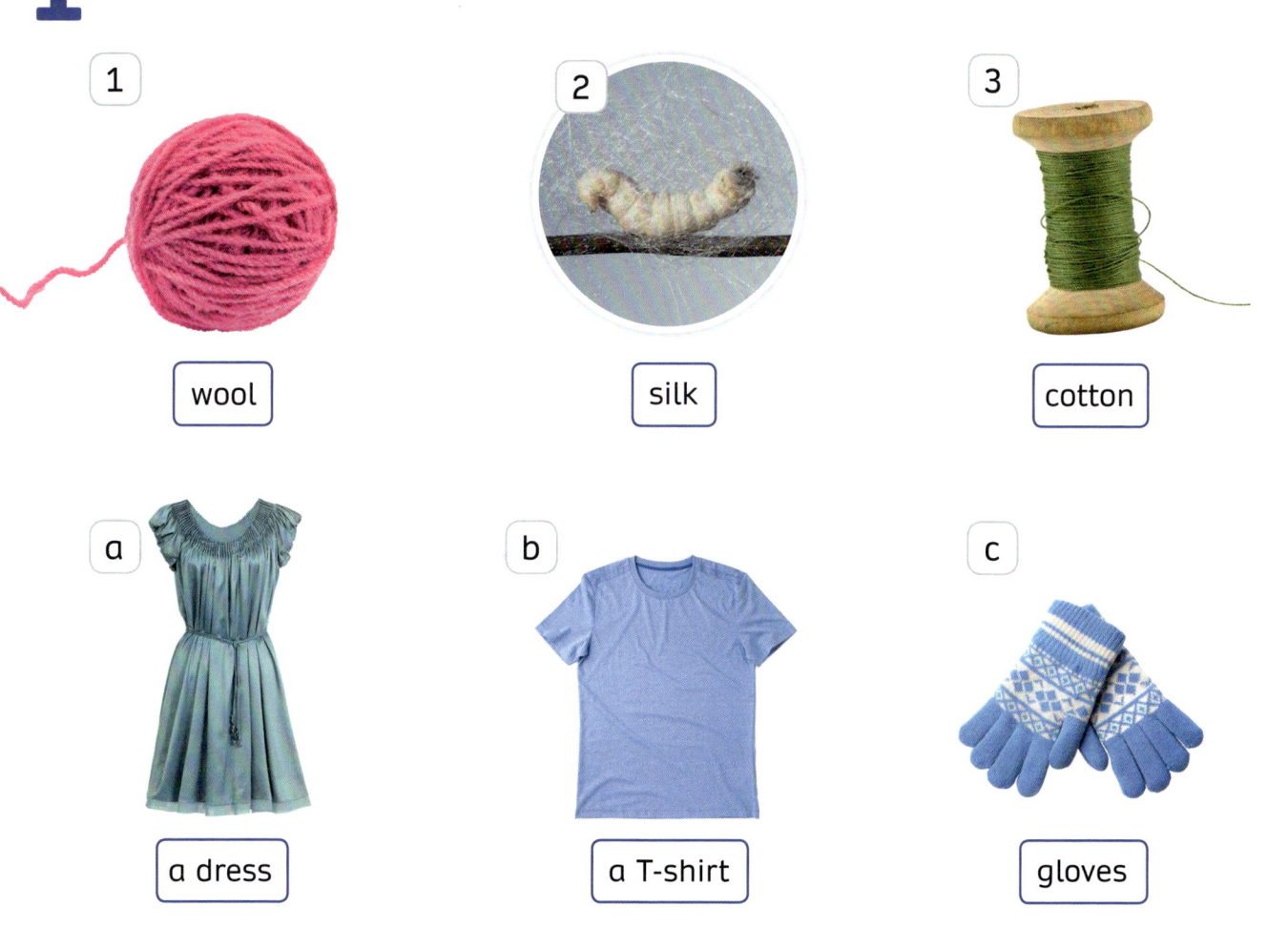

1 wool

2 silk

3 cotton

a a dress

b a T-shirt

c gloves

Story 1

2 🎧 3-18 **Listen. Check your answers from Activity 1.**

What Are CLOTHES Made From?

Wool

I'm Adam. I'm wearing a wool sweater, a hat, and gloves.

3 🎧 3-19 **Listen and check (✓).**

1			
2			
3			
4			
5			
6			

4 💬 **Talk about your clothes in pairs.**

This is my T-shirt. It's cotton.

This is my sweater. It's wool.

152

Silk

Lin is wearing a beautiful silk dress.

Cotton

I'm Tomas and this is Maria. She's wearing a red T-shirt.

Grammar 1

1  10-2 **Watch Parts 1 and 2 of the story video. Circle.**

Dan is wearing a pink
hat / sweater.

2 3-20 **Listen. Read and repeat.**

Grammar

🙂

I**'m wearing** a T-shirt.
You**'re wearing** a T-shirt.
He**'s wearing** a T-shirt.

🙁

I**'m not wearing** a blouse.
You **aren't wearing** a blouse.
She **isn't wearing** a blouse.

3 **Read and match. Then say.**

1

2

3

a He's wearing
a blue jacket.

b They aren't
wearing yellow
T-shirts.

c She isn't wearing
yellow sneakers.

4 **Complete for you and your friend.**

| isn't | 'm | 'm not | 's |

1 I .... wearing a skirt.

2 I .... wearing pants.

3 My friend .... wearing a sweater.

4 My friend .... wearing shoes.

Listening and Speaking

5   **Listen and circle.**

3-21

1

Marc

Antonio

2

Zehra

Lola

6   **Describe the pictures with a friend.**

He's wearing socks.

It's Marc.

155

Vocabulary 2

1 **Listen and repeat.**
3-22

dry | wet | warm | cool

thick | thin | short | tall

2 **Listen and number.**
3-23

3  **Listen and say.**
3-24

4 **Trace and write the opposites.**

thick   *short*

wet   *cool*

dry	....
....	tall
warm	....
....	thin

5 **Think. What are the opposites?**

- big
- young

6 Imagine and write.

| a cotton T-shirt | a rain jackets | a thick sweater |
| rain boots | sandals | wool gloves |

1   I'm wearing ...

... to be cool.

2   I'm wearing ...

... to be warm.

3   I'm wearing ...

... to be dry.

Story 2

1 Look at the picture. Check (✓).

He's a ...

doctor ☐   soldier ☐

He's wearing ...

a jacket ☐   pants ☐

shorts ☐   boots ☐

sandals ☐   a hat ☐

Story 2

2 3-25 Listen to the story. Check your answers from Activity 1.

Oscar's Day at the Palace

3  3-26 **Listen and check (✓).**

1

3

5

2

4

4 **Think about the story. Talk in pairs.**

Grammar 2

1 10-3  **Watch Part 3 of the story video. Whose pink dress is it?**

> Dan! Are you wearing my dress?

2 3-27 **Listen. Read and repeat.**

Grammar

Are you **wearing** a dress? **Yes**, I **am**./**No**, I'**m not**.

Is he **wearing** a T-shirt? **Yes**, he **is**./**No**, he **isn't**.

Is she **wearing** a T-shirt? **Yes**, she **is**./**No**, she **isn't**.

3 3-28 **Listen and check (✓) or cross (✗).**

1

2

3

4

4 Look at the pictures in Activity 3. Match.

1. Is Dan wearing a dress?
2. Is Cranky wearing a sweater?
3. Is Suzie wearing sandals?
4. Is Suzie wearing a skirt?

a. No, he isn't.
b. Yes, she is.
c. No, she isn't.
d. Yes, he is.

5 Answer for you. ❓

> No, I'm not.   Yes, I am.

Are you wearing …

1. a shirt? ....
2. a sweater? ....
3. a bathing suit? ....

4. a blouse? ....
5. a skirt? ....
6. gloves? ....

Speaking

6 💬 Complete the chart for you. Then ask two friends.

	sweater	T-shirt	shorts	sandals
Me				

Are you wearing a sweater?

Are you wearing a T-shirt?

Yes, I am.

No, I'm not.

Phonics

1 🎧 3-29 **Listen and repeat. Then trace.**

2 🎧 3-30 **Listen and match. Then say the words.**

v w

3 🎧 3-31 **Which sound do you hear? Circle *v* or *w*.**

1 v w   **2** v w   **3** v w   **4** v w

4 **Draw and write.**

w

v

Now I Know

1 **What clothes do we wear? Read and think.**

① at school? ....
② for sport? ....
③ for swimming? ....

④ to a party? ....
⑤ to be warm? ....
⑥ to be dry? ....

2 **Choose a project.**

UNIFORM

or

CLOTHES

★ ★ ★ ★ Color the stars ★ ★ ★ ★

 I can identify someone from a description.

 I can talk about what people are wearing.

 I can read new words in short, simple sentences.

 I can write simple clothes words.

Why do we travel?

Listening
- I can understand what people are doing.

Reading
- I can understand short, simple sentences about everyday activities.

Speaking
- I can ask simple questions about traveling.

Writing
- I can write simple words related to traveling.

1 Look out of the window. What can you see? Check (✓).

2 Look at the picture. Talk in pairs.

3 11-1 BBC Watch the video and circle. What can you see?

a boat   a bus

a plane   a train

Vocabulary 1

1 🎧 3-32 **Listen and complete. Then listen again and repeat.**

helicopter

motorcycle

subway

b ....

t ....

drive

ride

fly

sail

2 🎧 3-33 **Listen and say.**

3 💡 **Look at the words in Activity 1 and write.**

Drive

Ride

Sail

Fly

4 Complete for you.

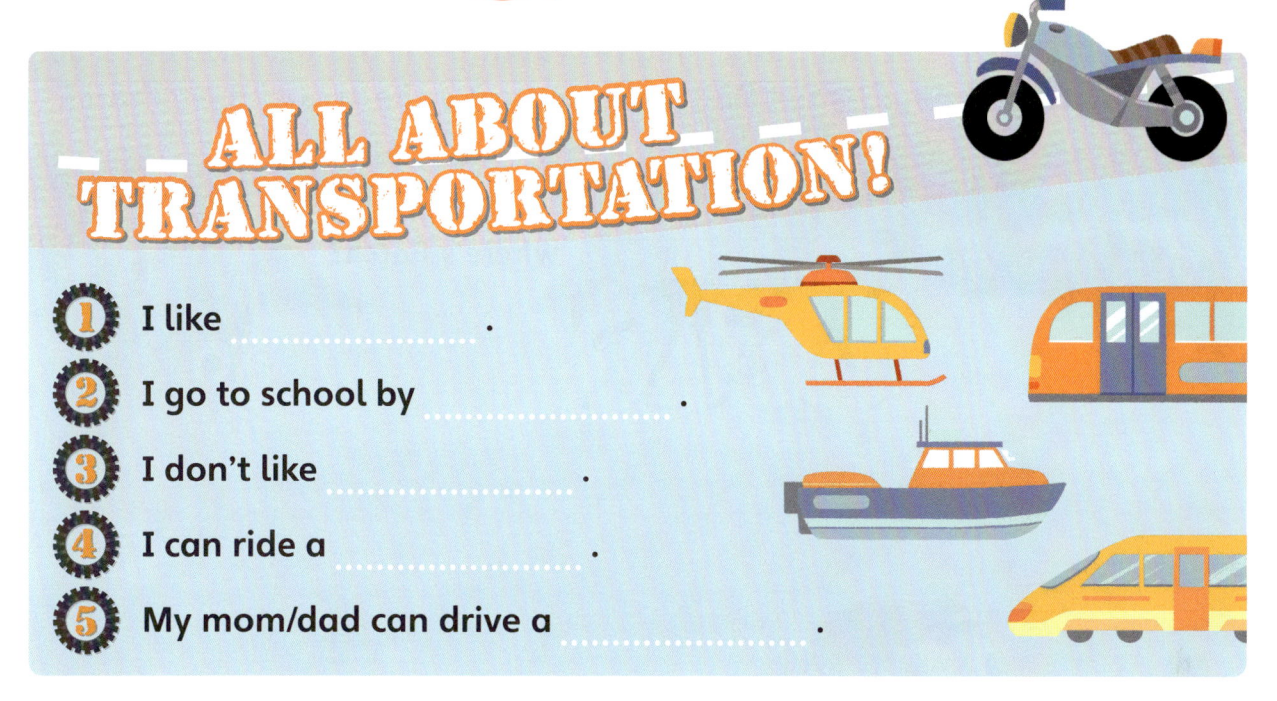

ALL ABOUT TRANSPORTATION!

1. I like ....
2. I go to school by ....
3. I don't like ....
4. I can ride a ....
5. My mom/dad can drive a ....

Story 1

1 Look at the pictures. Talk in pairs.

2 Read. What's the story about? Check (✓) the pictures in Activity 1.

Alicia and her family are on **vacation**.

Patch's Journey

Alicia and her family are on vacation. Patch is Alicia's stuffed animal. He's on vacation, too! It's their last day, and they're walking on the beach. "Let's go, Alicia. It's time to go home," says Dad. "We can take the **train** to the hotel."

Oh, no, where's Patch?

This isn't a fish!

Story 1

3 🎧 3-34 Listen to the story. Check your answers from Activity 2.

4 🎧 3-35 Listen again. Number *Patch's Journey* in order.

11

What are you doing there, Patch?

5 **Think about the story. Talk in pairs.**

How do you like to travel?

I like to travel by boat.

Grammar 1

1  **Watch Parts 1 and 2 of the story video. Where's Cranky?**

Cranky is driving a ....

2 **Listen. Read and repeat.**

Grammar

🙂

I**'m** rid**ing** a bike.

She**'s**/He**'s** watch**ing** TV.

You/We/They**'re** hav**ing** lunch.

🙁

I**'m not** play**ing**.

He/She **isn't** swimm**ing**.

You/We/They **aren't** draw**ing**.

---

3 **Read and check (✓) or cross (✗).**

1 They're riding a bike.

3 He's swimming.

2 He's sailing in a boat.

4 He's walking on the beach.

4 Choose and write the words.

1 Mary and Kate .... a kite. (fly)

2 Marco .... a scooter. (ride)

3 Ayan and Tina .... on the monkey bars. (play)

4 Mei .... (run)

Speaking 1

5 Play with a friend.

> The hippos are driving a truck.

> No, they aren't. They're driving a car.

6 11-3 **BBC** Watch Part 3 of the story video.
Does Dan like boats?

Vocabulary 2

1 🎧 3-37 **Listen and chant. Then complete and say.**

10	20	30	40	50	60	70	80	90	100
20	....	....	23	24	....	26	....	28	....

2 🎧 3-38 **Listen and repeat.**

safe

dangerous

fast

slow

modern

old-fashioned

3 🎧 3-39 **Listen and number.**

4 🎧 3-40 **Listen and say the opposites.**

5 💡 **Trace and match.** ❓

1 safe
2 dangerous
3 old-fashioned
4 modern
5 fast
6 slow

a
b
c
d
e
f

6  **Listen and circle.**

3-41

1

a
35 / 55

b
35 / 62

2

a
48 / 28

b
77 / 28

3

a
59 / 21

b
29 / 59

Story 2

1 **Look at the pictures. What places can you see?**

Story 2

2 🎧 3-42 **Listen to the story. Check your answers from Activity 1.**

What Is a JOURNEY?

Alex lives in Barcelona and he walks to school. He lives in a **modern** flat near his school in a busy street.

3 🎧 3-43 **Listen again. Circle the answers.**

1 Alex **walks** / **rides** to school.

2 Lilly goes by **train** / **bus**.

3 Javier goes by **car** / **helicopter**.

Lilly lives on a farm in Australia. She has to go by school bus to school.

Javier lives in Buenos Aires. His mum drives him to school every day.

4 🗨 **Do a survey about how your friends get to school.**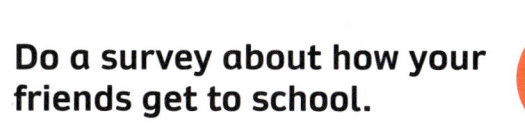

How do you get to school?

I get to school by bus.

Grammar 2

1 **11-3** BBC **Watch Part 3 of the story video again. Look and write.**

1

We can go to the
....

2

We can go by
....

3

We can go by
....

2 **3-44** **Listen. Read and repeat.**

Grammar

We **can go to the** beach!   We **can go on** foot.
We **can go by** car/bike/train.   We **can walk**/**run**/**fly**.

3 **3-45** **Listen and travel through the maze.**

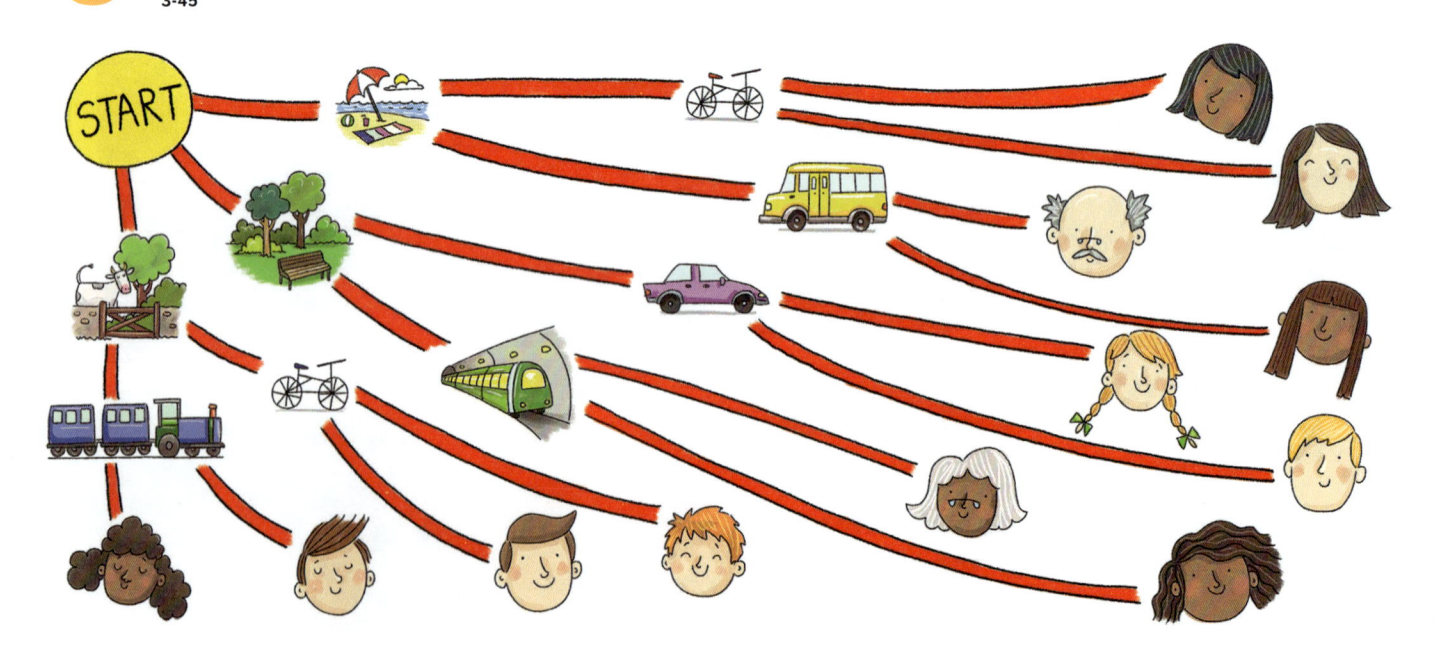

4 **Look and complete.**

> How **can** we go to the beach?
>
> 😊 We _____ go by bus.
>
> 🙁 We _____ go by bike.

5 💬 **How can you go to school? Ask and answer in pairs.**

	On foot	By bus	By taxi	By bike	By subway	Other
Me						
My friend						

Speaking 2

6 💬 **Play a game in pairs.**

How can we go
to the park?

We can go
by bike.

Phonics

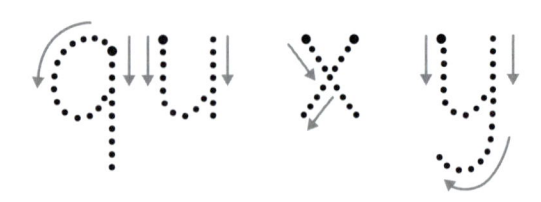

1 🎧 3-46 **Listen and repeat. Then trace.**

2 🎧 3-47 **Listen and match. Then say the words.**

   **y** **qu**

3 🎧 3-48 **Listen and check (✓) the words you hear. Where's the _x_ sound?**

1  ☐  ☐

2  ☐  ☐

3  ☐  ☐

4 🎧 3-49 **Listen and write. How many foxes?**

5 **Draw and write.**

y   qu   x

....

11

Now I Know

1 **Why do you travel? Think and circle.**

to visit people

to visit places

to go on vacation

to go to school

2 **How do you travel? Write.**

By .... On ....

3 **Choose a project.**

A family vacation.

or

A transportation poster.

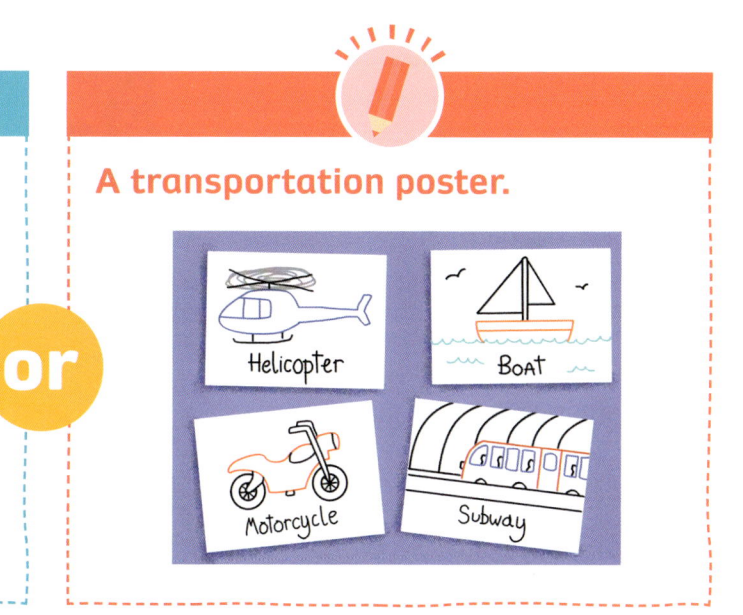

Color the stars

 I can understand what people are doing.

 I can ask simple questions about traveling.

 I can understand short, simple sentences about everyday activities.

 I can write simple words related to traveling.

12

Where do we live?

Listening
- I can understand simple conversations about everyday activities.

Reading
- I can read simple sentences about homes.

Speaking
- I can ask simple questions about homes.

Writing
- I can write simple words and sentences about homes.

1 What rooms do you know in English? Circle.

bedroom

bathroom

kitchen

living room

dining room

2  Look at the picture. Talk in pairs.

3 12-1 BBC Watch the video and circle. What room do they make?

a bathroom   a bedroom

a living room

4 12-1 BBC Watch the video again and check (✓).

a bed	☐	a chair	☐
a computer	☐	a TV	☐
a table	☐	a window	☐

Vocabulary 1

1 Listen and repeat.
3-50

bathtub refrigerator stove lamp

couch bookcase closet sink

2 Listen and number.
3-51

3 Listen and say.
3-52

4 What is it? Write and match.

1 You sit on it.
2 You put clothes in it.
3 You put cheese in it.
4 You take a bath in it.
5 You cook on it.
6 You use it to read.

a ....

b

c ....

d ....

e ....

f

....

....

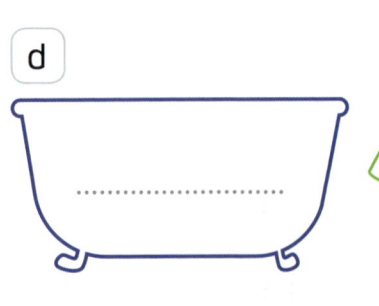

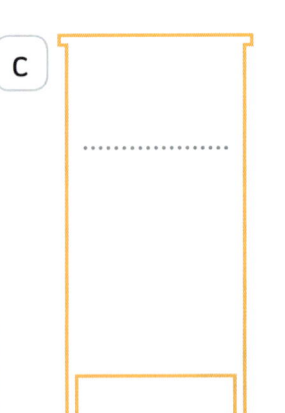

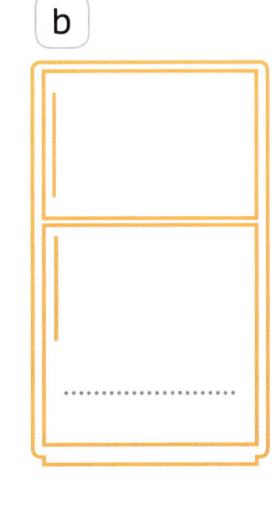

5 Look and sort.

> bathtub   bookcase   closet   couch
> lamp   refrigerator   sink   stove

bathroom

....

....

living room

....

....

....

bedroom

....

....

....

kitchen

....

....

Story 1

1 **Look at the pictures. Where do you think they live? Match.**

1  I sleep in a hammock.

2  My mom cooks on this stove.

3  This is my couch.

a

b

c

Story 1

2 3-53 **Listen to the story. Check your answers from Activity 1.**

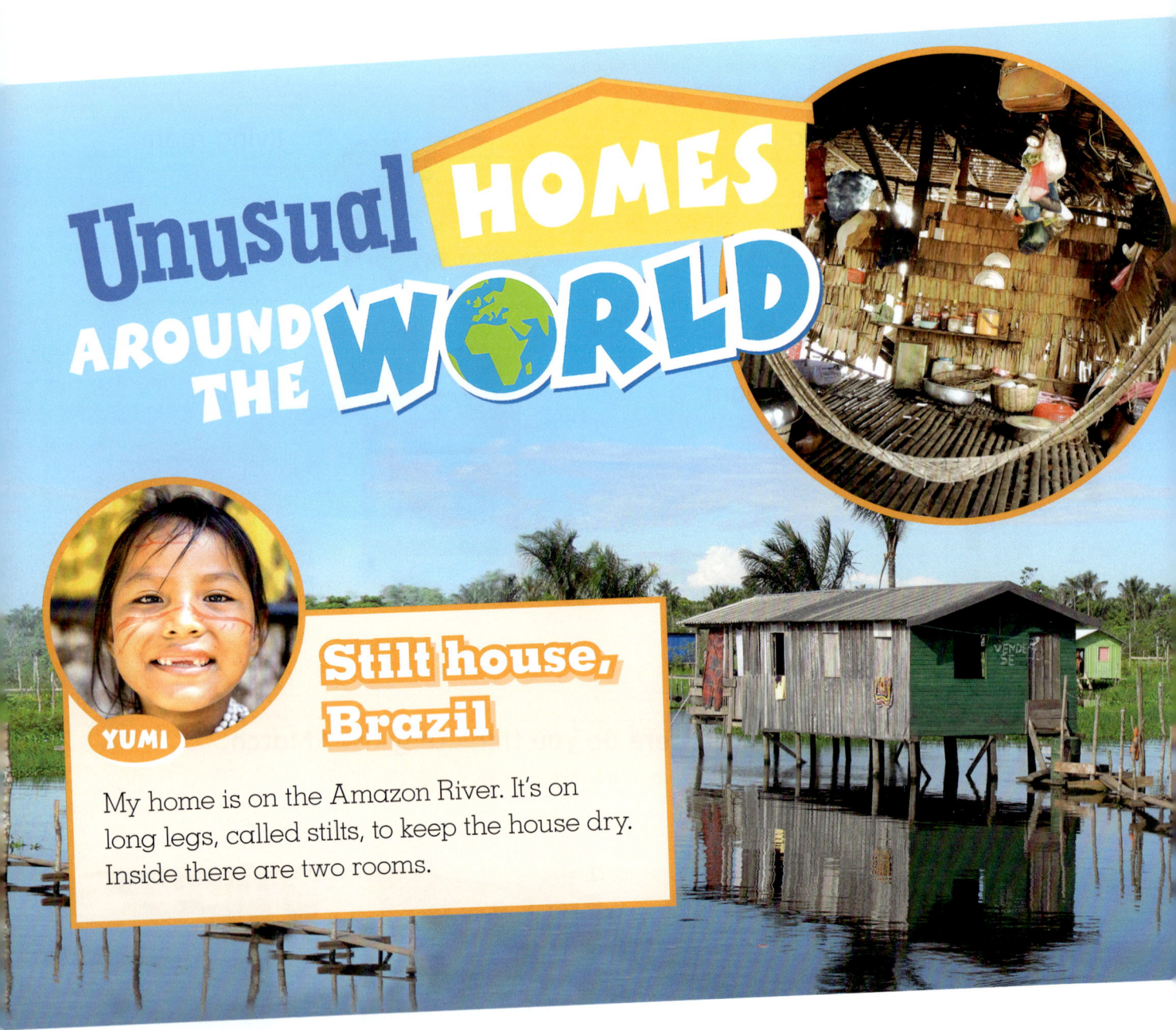

Unusual HOMES AROUND THE WORLD

YUMI

Stilt house, Brazil

My home is on the Amazon River. It's on long legs, called stilts, to keep the house dry. Inside there are two rooms.

3 3-54 **Listen again. Write *Y* (Yumi), *S* (Sarnai), or *I* (Izem).**

1 My home is underground. ......
2 My home is round. ......
3 My home is on legs. ......

4 I wash in the river. ......
5 There's a stove in the middle. ......
6 There are four rooms. ......

Ger, Mongolia

I live with my family in a ger. It's a small, round house with one room. We eat, sleep, and cook in this room.

SARNAI

IZEM

Underground home, Tunisia

It's very hot in my country, so I live under the ground. It isn't hot under the ground – it's cool. My house has four rooms.

4  **Talk in pairs. Imagine you live in one of** these homes. **?**

My home is on the river.

There are two rooms.

There isn't a bathtub.

You sleep in a hammock.

Grammar 1

1   **Watch Parts 1 and 2 of the story video. What rooms do you hear?**

12-2

Is Cranky watching TV?

No, he isn't.

2 **Listen. Read and repeat.**

3-55

> ### Grammar
>
> **Are** you sleep**ing**? **Yes**, I **am**./**No**, I'm **not**.
>
> **Is** he watch**ing** TV? **Yes**, he **is**.
> **Is** she tak**ing** a shower? **No**, she **isn't**.
>
> Are they listen**ing** to music? **Yes**, they **are**./**No**, they **aren't**.

3 **Read and match.**

1 Cranky, are you cooking in the kitchen? a No, they aren't.
2 Is Suzie washing in the living room? b Yes, he is.
3 Is Tommy eating in the dining room? c No, she isn't.
4 Are they sleeping in the bathroom? d Yes, I am.

4 **Read and match. Then listen.**
3-56

What	do you go to bed?
Where	many brothers do you have?
Who	are you wearing?
When	do you live with?
How	do you live?

5 **Look at Activity 4. Ask and answer with a friend.**

> Where do you live?

> I live in an apartment.

Listening and Speaking

6 **Listen and check (✓).**
3-57

	 watch TV	do your homework	 listen to music	 eat breakfast
bathroom				
living room				
kitchen				
bedroom				

7  **Where do you … ? Ask and answer.**

> Where do you watch TV?

> I watch TV in the living room.

Vocabulary 2

1 3-58 **Listen and repeat.**

2 3-59 **Listen and number.**

.... house

.... townhouse

.... apartment

.... cottage

.... palace

.... trailer

.... barge

.... tree house

3 3-60 **Listen and circle. Then say.**

1 My home is a big **palace** / **house**.

3 Mark lives in a **townhouse** / **tree house**.

2 I live in a **trailer** / **barge**.

4 Jaime lives in **a cottage** / **an apartment**.

188

4 Read the descriptions. Complete.

> barge   cottage   palace   tree house

1
This home is very big. The Queen lives here. It's a ....

3
This home is a kind of boat. It's a ....

2
This home is in the yard. It's a ....

4
This home is small and old. It's a ....

Story 2

1 Look and match.

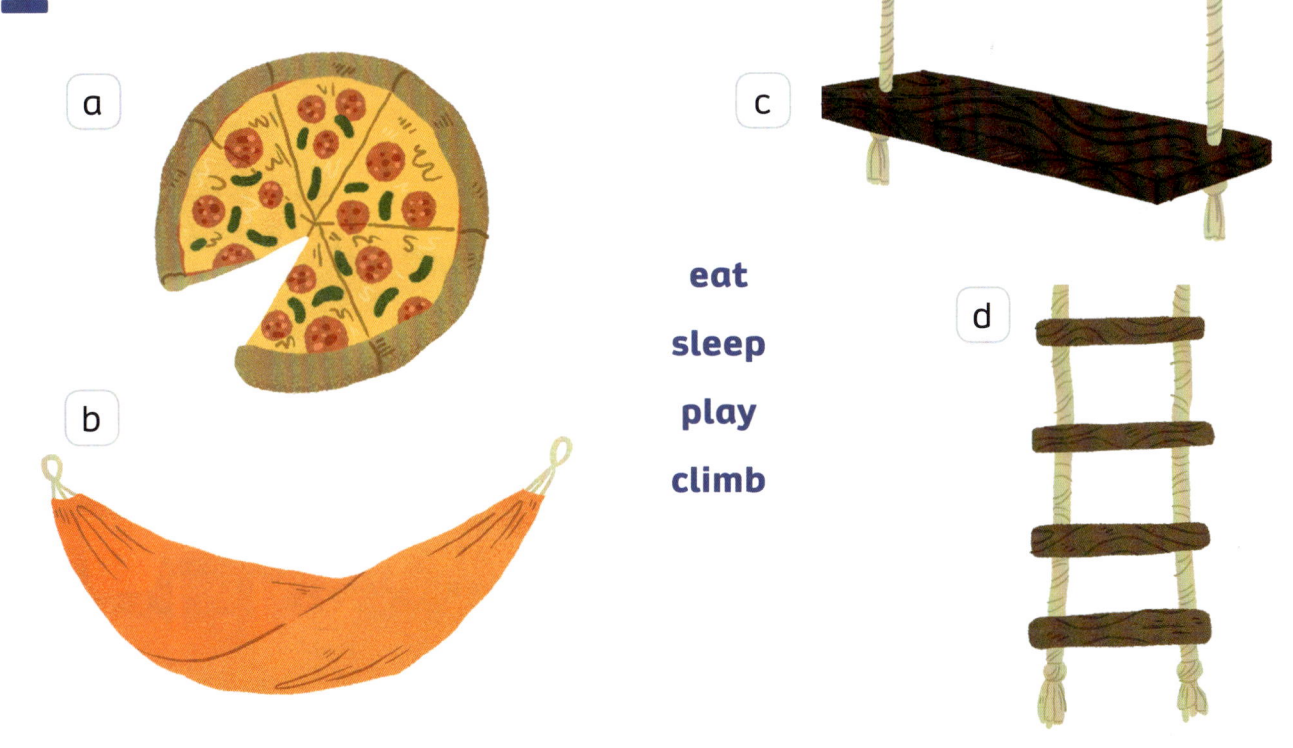

a

c

eat

sleep

play

climb

b

d

2 Look at Activity 1. What home do you think the story is about? Circle.

a palace   a barge   a tree house   a house

Story 2

The Tree House

Daniel lives in a **house**. But his favorite place is his **tree house** in the yard. It's his very own **palace**.

Daniel's friend, Maria lives in a **townhouse**. "Maria. Do you like my tree house?" asks Daniel.

"Yes!" says Maria. "And I like the swings under the tree house! Let's play!"

4  3-62 **Listen again. Number the sentences in order.**

 ...... They go home for ice cream.

 ...... They eat pizza.

 *1* They play on the swings.

 ...... The bell rings.

5 💬 **Close your book. Tell the story to a friend.**

6 💡 **Think about the story. Compare your ideas.**

Grammar 2

1   **Watch Part 2 of the story video. Where's the couch? Circle.**

bathroom   bedroom   kitchen

2 **Listen. Read and repeat.**
3-63

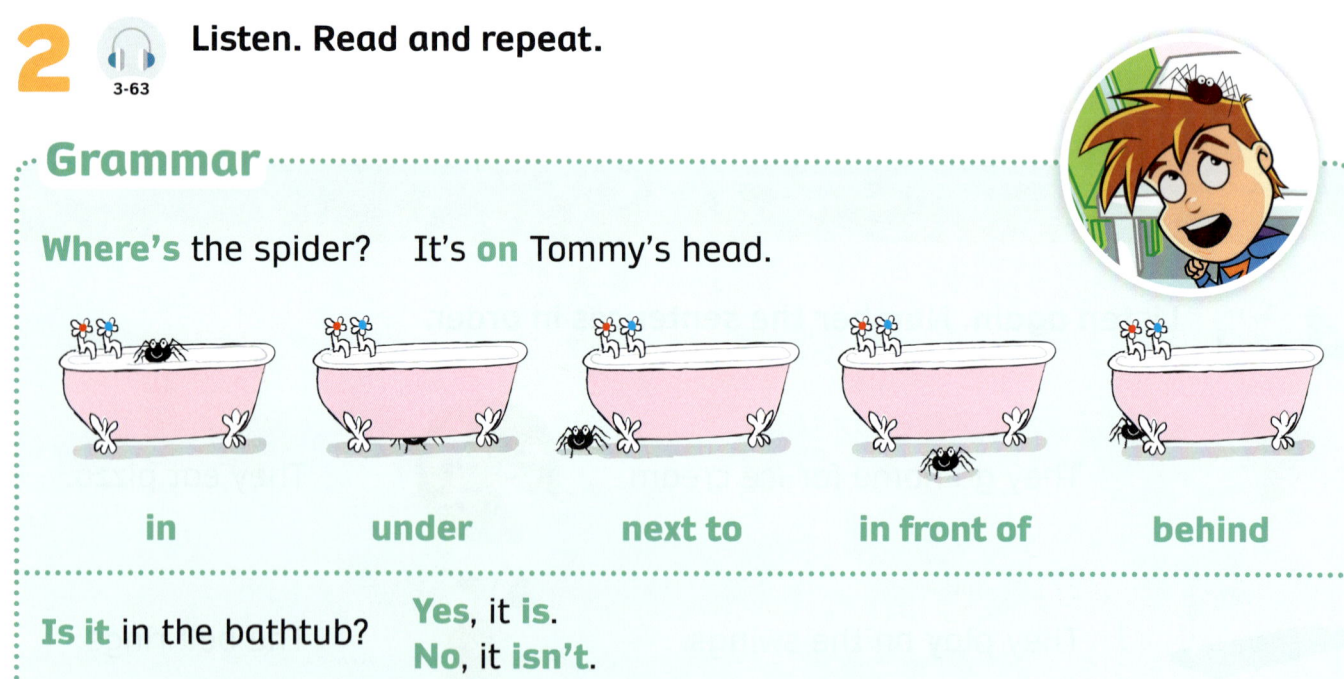

Grammar

Where's the spider?   It's **on** Tommy's head.

| in | under | next to | in front of | behind |

Is it in the bathtub?   **Yes**, it **is**.
No, it **isn't**.

3 **Look at the picture in Activity 1. Read and circle.**

The couch is **behind** / **next to** the refrigerator.

4   12-2  **Watch Part 2 of the story video again. Match.**

1   Where's the bathtub?   a   It's in the kitchen.

2   Where's the couch?   b   It's in the bedroom.

3   Where's the table?   c   It's in the living room.

4   Where's the blue lamp?   d   It's in the bathroom.

5   **Look at the picture in Activity 1. Answer the questions.**

1   Is it in the bathroom?

No, it isn't. It's _____ the _____ .

2   Is it under the refrigerator?

_____ .

3   Is it next to the refrigerator?

_____ . It's _____ the refrigerator.

 Where's the blue couch?

Speaking

6  **Ask and answer about your home.** ?

Where's the bookcase? Is it in the bathroom?

No, it isn't! It's in the living room. It's behind the couch.

 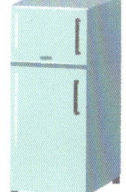  

7 12-3 BBC **Watch Part 3 of the story video. Does Cranky like his home?**

Phonics

1 🎧 3-64 **Listen and repeat. Then trace.**

2 🎧 3-65 **Listen. Check (✓) the pictures with words that begin with z.**

3 🎧 3-66 **Listen and repeat. Then trace.**

4 🎧 3-67 **Listen. Match the ss words and the zz words.**

194

Now I Know

1  **Where do we live? Think about your home. Draw and write.**

I live in a _____ .

There are _____ rooms.

I _____ in the living room.

In my bedroom, there's a _____ and a _____ .

2 **Choose a project.**

Design an unusual home.

This is my palace. It's very big.

or

Design your own tree house.

I play in my tree house.
I play on my swing.

★ ★ ★ ★ **Color the stars** ★ ★ ★ ★

 I can understand simple conversations about everyday activities.

 I can ask simple questions about homes.

 I can read simple sentences about homes.

 I can write simple words and sentences about homes.

Wordlist

Unit 1

Key vocabulary

cafeteria
computer lab
desk
draw
glue stick
library
markers
pen
pencil sharpener
playground
read
ruler
speak
tablet
whiteboard
write

Revised Vocabulary

backpack
book
chair
classroom
crayon
eraser
listen
Miss
number
pencil
school
sing
sit down
stand up
teacher

Unit 2

Key vocabulary

bird
brown
butterfly
circle
diamond
fish
gray
heart
orange
pink
purple
rectangle
side
square
star
triangle

Revised Vocabulary

big
black
blue
boat
door
green
kite
playground
red
small
train
white
yellow

Unit 3

Key vocabulary

afternoon
brush my teeth
dinnertime
do homework
evening
get up
go to bed
go to school
lunchtime
night
noon
play sports
play video games
sunrise
sunset
take a shower

Revised Vocabulary

breakfast
dinner
drink
eat
lunch
morning
night
park
sleep
wash
watch TV

Unit 4

Key vocabulary

barn
bee
calf
duck
duckling
eggs
goat

goose
honey
kid
kitten
lamb
meat
milk
nest
puppy
sheep

Revised Vocabulary

baby
big
bird
cat
chicken
cow
dog
farm
fish
happy
rabbit
small

Unit 5

Key vocabulary

aunt
daughter
grandparents
help
laugh
live together
noisy
old
parents
quiet
share
son
talk
twins
uncle
young

Revised Vocabulary

brother
cousin
dad
grandma
grandpa
mom
sister

Unit 6

Key vocabulary

bend
blond
dance
dark
finger
kick
knee
long
round
short
smile
snap
spin
step
toes
wave

Revised Vocabulary

arm
body
clap
ear
eye
face
foot
hair
hand
head
leg
mouth
nose
point
stamp

Unit 7

Key vocabulary

board game
climb
code
computer
game
hobby
hop
phone
ride a bike
screen
skip
soccer
sports
swim
take pictures
type

Revised Vocabulary

arms
dance
ears
eyes
favorite
feet
head
legs
mouth
tablet
walk

Unit 8

Key vocabulary

beans
bread
carrot
cookies
grapes
lemon
lime
onion

pasta
pear
peas
pineapple
potato
rice
soup
yogurt

apple
banana
cheese
ice cream
meat
milk
orange
picnic
water

Unit 9

Key vocabulary

action figure
blocks
hopscotch
hula-hoop
lose
monkey bars
robot
scooter
slide
stuffed animal
swings
tag
take turns
toy boat
toy truck
win

Revised Vocabulary

ball
bike
board game
car
doll
kite
plane
teddy bear

Unit 10

Key vocabulary

bathing suit
blouse
boots
cool
dry
gloves
jacket
sandals
short
shorts
sweater
tall
thick
thin
warm
wet

Revised Vocabulary

colours
dress
jeans
pants
shirt
shoe
skirt
socks
T-shirt

Unit 11

Key vocabulary

boat
dangerous
drive
fast
fly
helicopter
modern
motorcycle
numbers 20-100
old-fashioned
ride
safe
sail
slow
subway
train

Revised Vocabulary

bike
plane

Unit 12

Key vocabulary

apartment
barge
bathtub
behind
bookcase
closet
cottage
couch
house
in
in front of
lamp
next to
on
palace
refrigerator
sink

stove
townhouse
trailer
tree house
under

Revised Vocabulary

bathroom
bedroom
dining room
house
kitchen
living room
table